100 WARS

THAT SHAPED WORLD HISTORY

Samuel Willard Crompton

A Bluewood Book

This edition produced and published in 1997 by Bluewood Books
A Division of The Siyeh Group, Inc.,
P.O. Box 689
San Mateo, CA 94401

ISBN 0-912517-28-X

Printed in USA
10, 9, 8, 7, 6, 5, 4, 3, 2

Designed by Eric Irving
Copy Edited by Linnea Due
Edited by Barbara Krystal
Cover illustration by Tony Chikes

About the Author:

Samuel Willard Crompton teaches American and European history at Holyoke Community College in Massachusetts. Keenly interested in American biography, he has served as a Writing Fellow for the *American National Biography* (Oxford University Press, 1998) and contributed many sections to the *Cambridge Dictionary of American Biography* (Cambridge University Press, 1995). He holds degrees from Framingham State College and Duke University. A free-lance writer for over ten years, he is the author of *100 Battles that Shaped World History* (Bluewood Books, 1997), and *Presidents of the United States* (Smithmark, 1992). An avid bicyclist and traveler, he has seen much of North America by plane, train, car, and foot. Long interested in public service, he has been a tax preparer and telephone operator. He lives in western Massachusetts, a rural region that has produced many remarkable Americans, including Cecil B. DeMille and Russell H. Conwell, and has served as poetic inspiration for many others, including Archibald MacLeish and Richard Wilbur.

Picture Acknowledgements:
Bluewood Books Archives: all pages except;
U.S. Library of Congress: 83, 85, 89, 91, 105, 107
U.S. National Archives: 77, 84, 86, 88, 93, 94, 95, 96, 97, 99, 100, 101
National Army Museum: 83, 85
U.S. Naval Institute: 61
Illustrations by Tony Chikes: 92, 98, 102, 103, 104, 106

TABLE OF CONTENTS

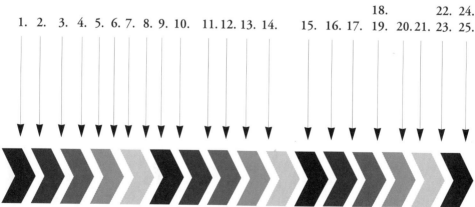

1. 2. 3. 4. 5. 6. 7. 8. 9. 10. 11. 12. 13. 14.   15. 16. 17. 18. 19. 20. 21. 22. 24. 23. 25.

600 BC   **1200 AD**

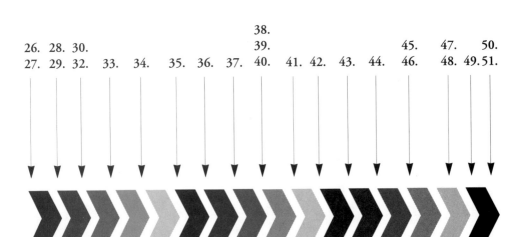

26. 28. 30.
27. 29. 32. 33. 34. 35. 36. 37. 38.
                                     39.   45.   47.   50.
                                     40. 41. 42. 43. 44. 46.   48. 49.51.

1200 AD   4   **1780 AD**

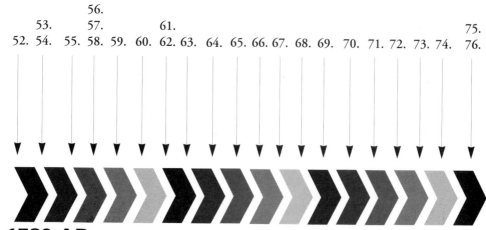

53. 56. 57. 61. 75.
52. 54. 55. 58. 59. 60. 62. 63. 64. 65. 66. 67. 68. 69. 70. 71. 72. 73. 74. 76.

1780 AD **1880 AD**

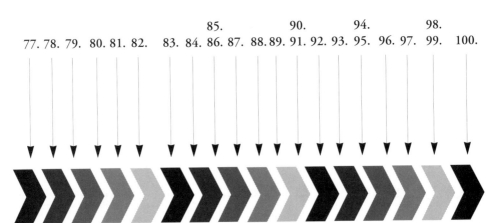

INTRODUCTION

From the remarkable conquests of **Cyrus the Great** of Persia to the American victory in the **Persian Gulf War**, mankind has shown a marked tendency to engage in warfare between tribes, religions, nations and states. Certain rivalries spring to mind: Trojans versus Greeks, British against French, Communist nations versus capitalist, and in recent times, Arabs against Israelis.

"A prince should therefore have no other aim or thought, nor take up any other thing for his study, but war and its organization and discipline, for that is the only art that is necessary to one who commands."

So says Niccolo Machiavelli, in 1532's The Prince, indicating that even during the heyday of the Italian Renaissance, famous for its artistic expression, men granted war priority as a primary instrument of national policy. A more recent example of war's hold on humankind: at the end of the nineteenth century, a great optimism arose, particularly among upper-class Europeans and Americans, that education, science, medicine, and the application of rational thought would eliminate war, disease, famine, and conflict in the century to come. Instead, the twentieth century has seen two enormous global wars, the development and use of atomic weapons, a striking resurgence in tribalism (in Europe especially), and a host of new diseases that may outdistance the best efforts of doctors and antibiotics. And even as the **Cold War** came to an end in 1990, the United States was organizing a multinational coalition to combat Iraq's **Saddham Hussein**. Predictions that war will someday be unnecessary seem ill-founded, and we are forced to ponder the possibility that each generation must confront its own evils.

"There never was a good war or a bad peace," said **Benjamin Franklin** in a letter to his friend, Josiah Quincy, days after he had signed the treaty ending the **Revolutionary War**. Franklin has been echoed by many, and during the twentieth century, a strong pacifist movement gained ground in the United States. As late as 1915, the most popular American song was "I didn't raise my boy to be a soldier," though it was replaced two years later by "Over There," which extolled the virtues of the Yanks while urging them to strike at the German Huns. During the 1930s, an isolationist policy swept the United States, and it took the Japanese attack on **Pearl Harbor** to bring the country into **World War II**.. In 1960, the American people were treated to a piece of remarkable irony, when President **Dwight Eisenhower** warned them of the dangers of the "military-industrial complex," which he and his administration had done more to enhance than any other. When the United States did have a man in the White House who held to some pacifist beliefs, like **Jimmy Carter**, the electorate later dismissed him as being weak-willed.

As the world population creeps toward of six billion persons, and as resources become more and more scarce, it seems likely that future wars may occur between First and Third World countries, between the developed and underdeveloped areas of the globe. The only remedy to future calamities lies in the capacity of mankind to create an outlet for aggression, and find a way to cage the nuclear beast. If we are to be less dire and pessimistic than Machiavelli, and more realistic than Franklin. Before we can change the course of current events, we must understand what has come before. That is why we seek to learn about the wars that shaped world history.

His origins obscure, **Cyrus II** (Sigh-rus) (**c. 600-529 BC**) became the greatest leader of the ancient world prior to **Alexander the Great (356-323 BC)**. Probably born on the great plateau of what is now Iran, Cyrus became king of both the **Persians** and the **Medes** by 559 BC. Ruling over two distinct ethnic groups of fierce mounted warriors, Cyrus decided to expand his kingdoms at the expense of other peoples in the Middle East: the Lydians, Bactrians, Babylonians, and others.

The first of Cyrus' known wars was against King **Croesus** of Lydia, in present-day Turkey in 547-546 BC. The expression "rich as Croesus" comes from the fact that Lydia was the first kingdom known to mint coins and maintain an official treasury. Croesus is reputed to have consulted the oracle at **Delphi** in Greece, asking whether he should challenge Cyrus. The ambiguous answer he received was that if he attacked Cyrus, a great empire would be destroyed. Croesus went forth full of confidence, launched a war against Cyrus, and soon found that the empire destroyed was his own.

Cyrus established his capital city at **Susa** in present-day Iran. In 539 BC he went to war with the **Babylonian Empire**, centered on the city of Babylon on the Euphrates river. Cyrus captured **Babylon** after a long siege, ending nearly 1,500 years of continuous rule by the Babylonians over Mesopotamia, known as the land between the rivers, because it lay between the **Tigris** and **Euphrates** rivers in present-day Iraq. Cyrus also freed the thousands of Hebrews who had been brought to Babylon as captives by King **Nebuchadnezzar** 70 years earlier.

As king of the **Persian Empire**, and conqueror of Lydia and Babylon, Cyrus held a position never before attained: lord of all the land from the borders of India to the Mediterranean. His conquest of Babylon gave him control of the Phoenician fleet in present-day Lebanon. It is speculated that he set his sights on Egypt as his next conquest. Cyrus was killed while fighting against a tribe known as the **Massagetae**, on his eastern frontier. His tomb, erected at **Pasargadae**, contained the following inscription: "O man! Whosoever thou art and whensoever thou comest (for come I know thou wilt), I am Cyrus, the Founder of the Persian Empire. Envy me not the little earth that covers my remains." Cyrus had created an empire that would last 200 years, encompassing peoples as diverse as the Bactrians, Lydians, Egyptians, Phoenicians and Babylonians.

Cyrus the Great

2. GREEK-PERSIAN WARS
499-448 BC

Compared to the mighty **Persian Empire**, **Greece** was a small, insignificant land, dotted with small **city-states** each with a population of roughly 30,000. **Athens, Thebes, Sparta, Corinth** and other city-states generally did not cooperate with each other in times of peace; each tended to its own affairs and tried to outdo its neighbors in terms of trade. But this land of disunited political units needed assistance when the Persian Empire threatened to expand past **Turkey** and into the Aegean Sea.

In 499 BC, Greek colonies in Turkey began a revolt against Persian rule. Athens and other Greek city-states sent help to their fellow Greeks. In response, **Darius I (558-486 BC)** King of Persia, dispatched an army and fleet to conquer Greece in 490 BC.

The Persian fleet anchored off the Greek coast to the north of Athens. Some 30,000 Persian soldiers came ashore to march against Athens, the most exposed city to an attack by land and by sea. The Persians were attacked on the beach by 10,000 Athenians gathered on the heights above. Attacking on the run, the Greek hoplite warriors shattered the Persian center and caused the entire Persian army to retreat in disorder to its ships. Nearly 6,000 Persians lost their lives on the beach at **Marathon**, and Greece remained free, able to pursue its experiments in democracy.

Ten years later, **Xerxes** (Zhurk-sees) **(519-465 BC)**, who had succeeded Darius, made another attempt to subdue the Greeks. Leading 300,000 Persian soldiers by land

Spartans at Plataea

through Turkey, across the Hellespont, through Thrace, and into Greece, Xerxes reached Athens and burned large parts of the city in 480 BC. Soon after, however, he watched his fleet lose the battle of **Salamis**, just to the south of Athens. The Athenians had built new **trireme** vessels that carried three banks of oars; able to maneuver their ships more quickly in the restricted waters of the Bay of Salamis, the Greeks outfoxed the larger Persian fleet. Xerxes' large army depended on its fleet for supplies; he left Greece and returned to Asia, though he left behind a substantial army under the leader **Mardonius** to harass the Greeks the next year. Mardonius' army was completely defeated by the Greek **hoplite** warriors at **Plataea** in the spring of 479 BC.

Other skirmishes followed, and a lasting resentment developed on both sides. A renewal of the conflict seemed likely, but before taking on the Persians again, the Greeks would fight among themselves, in a series of conflicts known as the **Peloponnesian War** (see no. 3).

The Battle of Syracuse

Success can lead to arrogance, pride and vanity. Such seemed to be the case with Athens in the half-century following its defeat of the Persians at **Marathon**, **Salamis**, and **Plataea**. Flush from its naval victory at Salamis, Athens went on to develop an empire of its own in the **Aegean Sea**. Small islands soon found they had to pay tribute to Athens in order to maintain their status in the **Delian League**, an association meant to fend off future attacks from Persia. When one island, **Melos**, refused to pay tribute, the Athenians attacked the island, captured the inhabitants, and sold them into slavery. Other Greeks, whether Spartans, Corinthians or Thebans might well have wondered whether Athenian domination was better than a Persian takeover.

Sparta, a land-based power located in the southern part of Greece, emerged as the single greatest challenger to Athens. The Spartan warriors were known for their dedication and fearlessness. Following a series of diplomatic maneuvers and countermaneuvers, Athens and Sparta went to war, begining the long and vicious **Peloponnesian War**.

Led by **Pericles** (per-a-kleez) (**495-429 BC**), the Athenians refrained from meeting the Spartans in open combat. They allowed their enemy to ravage the vineyards around Athens, while they remained safe behind the walls of their city, and sent out fleets to harass Sparta by sea. This strategy proved sound for the first two years of the war, but then Athens was hit by a terrible plague that killed many of its best men, including Pericles. The war dragged on, with no end in sight.

Athens threw away great resources of men and money in a failed attempt to capture the city of **Syracuse**, Sicily, a Spartan ally. Meanwhile, the Spartans were developing a fleet of their own--with aid from Persia, the foe of all Greeks. They soon began to threaten the Athenian food supply. Totally dependent on grain brought to the city by ship from the **Black Sea**, the Athenians sailed forth to fight the Spartans. Sparta won the **Battle of Aegospotami** in 404 BC, effectively ending the war. Under the terms of the peace treaty, Athens was required to pull down its protective walls, to relinquish its maritime empire, and to allow for Spartan hegemony in Greece. Although the long war was over, other Greek city-states would come to resent Sparta as much as they had envied Athens.

4. GREEK CITY-STATES WARS
395-362 BC

Fighting among the Greek city-states resumed shortly after the **Peloponnesian War** (see no. 3) with city-states constantly jockeying for strategic alliances with one another. The Spartan defeat of **Athens** made their reputation and influence grow, but their heavy-handed domination of the peninsula of Greece prompted great resentment among the other city-states.

Conflict between Sparta and **Thebes**, once allies against Athens, erupted in 395 BC when **Lysander** marched a Spartan army to fight the **Boeotians** at **Hiliartus**. Theban forces joined the Boeotians in routing the Spartans and killing Lysander. This surprising victory gave life to the resistance against Spartan hegemony; but was short-lived when in 394 BC the Spartans defeated anti-Spartan forces at **Coronea** and then laid siege against **Corinth**. That same year a combined fleet of Persian and Athenian ships encountered 120 Spartan ships at **Cnidus** off the southwest coast of Asia Minor. The combined fleet won a decisive victory, delivering a severe blow to Sparta's command of the Aegean Sea. Another naval battle in 376 BC between Athens and Sparta at **Naxos** put another nail in Sparta's coffin.

The fall of Sparta and the rise of Thebes as the most powerful of city-states was decided at the **Battle of Leuctra** in 371 BC. Thebes had found a leader in **Epaminondas** (e-pam-i-non-das) **(418?-362 BC)**, the king's son. As a young boy, he had been sent to Sparta as a hostage, to guarantee the good behavior of his city-state of Thebes. During these years, he studied the Spartan military system. While admiring its discipline and steadfastness, Epaminondas noticed that the Spartans never varied their attacks; an observation that would serve him well on the battlefield at Leuctra.

Led by King **Cleombutrus I**, the Spartan army of 10,000 men invaded Theban territory and encountered a force of about 6,000 Thebans. Epaminondas had devised an effective tactic with which to fight the powerful Spartan **phalanx**. He had his best troops arranged 50 deep on his left flank, drawing his shallow and weaker center and right. This formation matched up against the usual Spartan formation of 8 to 12 deep across. The Spartans right flank gave way against the might of the Thebans left and a rout ensued. At the end of the battle Thebes stood supreme, but like Athens and Sparta before it, their might would inevitably be challenged. In 362 BC Epaminondas was killed in the **Battle of Mantinea**. With his demise, Thebes became leaderless and soon after collapsed.

The Battle of Leuctra

5. CONQUESTS OF ALEXANDER THE GREAT 334-323 BC

Alexander the Great (356-323 BC), son of **Philip of Macedon**, became king of Macedon in 336 BC. Seldom has a great military leader been succeeded by a son who proved even more skilled and ruthless in the arts of war. Almost from the day he attained the throne, Alexander the Great prosecuted war against any and all enemies; no one who challenged him escaped a confrontation.

The Greek city-state of **Thebes** resisted the rule of Alexander, saying he was too young. Alexander marched south, smashed the Theban army and demolished the city. That action quickly ended protest from the rest of the Greek city-states.

Following a long-held dream of his father, Alexander turned east toward **Asia Minor** (present-day Turkey) and the **Persian Empire** in 334 BC. He crossed the Hellespont with 30,000 Macedonian infantry and 5,000 cavalry. Though small in numbers, the Macedonian fighters were among the toughest and most ruthless of their day. They defeated far larger Persian armies at **Granicus**, **Miletus** and **Halicarnassus**. Alexander then advanced down the coast of the Mediterranean toward Egypt.

One city tried to hold out against him-- the Phoenician city of **Tyre**, located on an island half a mile off the coast. Alexander conducted a siege, hardly his favorite type of warfare. The siege dragged on from January through August 332 BC. The Tyrians held out, as they had ample water and their fleet to bring them supplies. Undaunted, Alexander had his men build a land bridge, a causeway, from the mainland to Tyre. The moment it was finished, he and his men sacked the city; all 30,000 inhabitants were sold into slavery.

Alexander went on to overwhelm the huge Persian army at **Arabela**. The glorious days of **Cyrus (600-529 BC)** and **Darius (558-486 BC)** were gone, and all of Persia soon succumbed to Alexander and his Macedonians. Alexander was a generous conqueror. He did not obliterate Persian culture, but sought to integrate it with Greek and Macedonian culture: to further this goal he once married 10,000 of his men to 10,000 Persian women in a mass ceremony.

Hungry for new glory, Alexander pushed east to **Bactria** and entered present-day Afghanistan and India. He fought his last large battle near the banks of the Indus River, then turned back because his soldiers refused to go further east. Furious at his men, Alexander led them through the arid **Gedrosian Desert** on the southern rim of Iran. He reached the famed city of **Babylon** in 323 BC and with no further land to conquer, died at the age of 32 after a bout of hard drinking. Supposedly, he answered the question of who should rule his empire, with the terse comment, "The strongest!"

Alexander the Great

6. FIRST PUNIC WAR
264-241 BC

The empire of **Alexander the Great (356-323 BC)** stretched eastward from Greece to India. Two other powers began to contest for supremacy in the central and western part of the Mediterranean Sea: **Rome** and **Carthage**. The former was a city-state formed on the banks of the **Tiber River** near the western coast of Italy, the latter a Phoenician city-state near present-day Tunis in North Africa. Both cities depended on trade, and both were very aggressive in staking out territorial claims. The two powers eventually clashed over who should have predominance on the island of **Sicily**, which lay in the Mediterranean between Rome and Carthage.

When the **First Punic War** began in 264 BC, Carthage held most of the advantages. Her fleet was large, and she had armies already positioned in Sicily. Within two years, Rome had built its first fleet (modeled after a captured Carthaginian trireme ship) and proceeded to win a series of important naval battles. The Romans fought the experience of the Carthaginian sailors with might: they brought many troops on their ships and when close to an enemy vessel, would drop a **corvus** (a ram with a spike at the end) onto the deck of their opponent. The corvus provided a narrow bridge across which Roman soldiers charged and fought, as if it were a land battle. Unnerved by the Romans' inventiveness and courage in hand-to-hand fighting, the Carthaginians evaded further naval battles with Rome, which gave control of the waters around Sicily to the new Roman legions.

Rome experienced one severe defeat in the war. A Roman army in North Africa was defeated, and its general, **Regulus**, was captured. Told by his Carthaginian captors to begin negotiations in order to save his life, Regulus instead informed his fellow Roman citizens they should fight on regardless of what might happen to him.

The war dragged on until 241 BC when the last Carthaginian soldiers in Sicily surrendered. In the peace treaty that followed, Rome imposed an indemnity upon Carthage, taking Sicily away from her permanently. To make matters worse, Carthage soon experienced a revolt by her unpaid mercenary soldiers. In the unstable times that followed, Rome took advantage of the situation and took **Sardinia** away from Carthage as well. Although Rome had won the first round of warfare with convincing certainty, she had not heard the last from her rival to the south. One of the Carthaginian generals, **Hamilcar Barca**, swore his four sons to an eternal hatred of Rome, and all four would eventually take up arms against their longtime enemy.

Regulus, the Roman Army General

SECOND PUNIC WAR
218-202 BC

Hannibal Barca

The Carthaginian thirst for revenge was personified by **Hannibal Barca (247-183 BC)** oldest of the four sons of **Hamilcar Barca**. Taught from an early age to hate Rome, Hannibal planned with his three brothers to strike at Rome in a place she was unlikely to expect--Spain. By 220 BC, the Barca brothers had set up a Carthaginian province in Spain, and in 219 BC they laid siege to the city of **Sanguntum**, an ally of Rome. Told by the Romans that they must cease or face a war, Hannibal captured Sanguntum.

Hannibal led 50,000 men out of Spain, into lower Gaul, crossed the Rhone River, and entered the **Alps**. The elephants he brought with him almost all died in the mountain crossings, but Hannibal and his men endured the trek to emerge in the **Po Valley** of northern Italy. Though they had suffered great losses to cold and hunger, Hannibal had recruited

men from the Gaulish tribes on his march.

Confident of repeating their successes in the **First Punic War**, the Romans sent army after army against Hannibal. The proud city of Rome was shocked when its troops were defeated at the Ticinus River in 218 BC, the Trebia River in 218 BC and at Lake Trasimere in 217 BC. Hannibal's crowning glory came at the **Battle of Cannae** in 216 BC, when he successfully executed a **double envelopment** maneuver, encircling and trapping 50,000 Roman soldiers on the field. The loss of its largest army and two of its consular leaders persuaded Rome to adopt different tactics. Under the leadership of **Fabian the Delayer**, Rome stayed on the defensive for years, biding its time until the moment came to strike back.

Rome's opportunity arrived when a new leader, **Publius Cornelius Scipio (237-183 BC)**, also known as **Afrikanus**, carried the war to Spain, defeating the Carthaginian forces there. **Hasdrubal Barca**, Hannibal's younger brother, led a second Carthaginian army over the Alps and into northern Italy, but that force was overwhelmed and crushed by Roman troops before Hannibal knew of his brother's proximity.

Flushed from his successes, Scipio crossed to Africa in 204 BC. He defeated several Carthaginian forces and made a crucial alliance with **Numidian** cavalrymen. Recalled to Africa to defend his homeland, Hannibal met Scipio at the **Battle of Zama** in 202 BC. Although Hannibal used every maneuver he could think of, the skill, professionalism, and confidence of Scipio's legions prevailed. Defeated, Hannibal urged the Carthaginian government to seek peace. Another indemnity was imposed on Carthage, with the African city-state swearing never to go to war again without Rome's permission.

Having disposed of the threat from Carthage in the **Second Punic War**, Rome turned its gaze eastward and soon ran into conflict with the **Kingdom of Macedonia.** The Macedonians had spawned the great warrior **Alexander the Great (356-323 BC)**. They were now confronted by the rising power of the Roman legions.

King **Perseus** of Macedon instigated an unsuccessful attempt on the life of **Eumenes II**, the king of **Pergamum.** Pergamum then declared war with Macedonia. Rome chose to support Pergamum, and sent an army under **P. Lucinius Crassus** to attack Macedonia by marching through Illyria in 171 BC. King Perseus defeated Crassus at the **Battle of Callicinus**, near present-day Larissa. The following year, Perseus repulsed another Roman army in Thessaly, this one led by **A. Hostilius Mancinus**. A third Roman invasion attempt under **Q. Marcius Phillippus** failed in 169 BC.

Knowing that King Perseus was attempting to bribe the Gallic tribes north of Macedonia to join him, Rome sent **Lucius Aemilius Paulus** to lead the Roman armies. Paulus found the dispirited Roman army encamped on the south bank of the Enipeus River, beside the shore of the Gulf of Thessalonika. He took two months to revitalize his troops, then set out to find and eliminate his foe.

Paulus sent part of his army around Mount Olympus in an attempt to surround the Macedonians. Perseus brought his men to a position beside the Aeson River, where they awaited the Romans. The night prior to the **Battle of Pydna** on June 21, 168 BC there was an eclipse of the moon, which inspired the Romans, but threw the Macedonians into consternation. When the battle began the next day, the Macedonian phalanx pushed back the Roman legions as long as the fighting was on solid ground. When the Romans perceived the Macedonian need for a level surface, they shifted their position, forcing the enemy to fight on uneven terrain. In the ensuing melee, the Romans killed 20,000 Macedonians and captured 12,000 others. Perseus escaped from the battlefield, but he later surrendered and died in captivity in Rome.

Macedonia was divided into four separate republics, all under the supervision of Rome. The Roman legion had decisively defeated the Greek phalanx, and Rome would soon refer to the Mediterranean as **Mare Nostrum** (Our Sea). The Roman victory was made complete when King **Attalus III** of Pergamum, son of Eumenes II, bequeathed the entire kingdom to Rome in 133 BC.

A Macedonian phalanx

9. THIRD PUNIC WAR
149-146 BC

Within fifty years of the end of the **Second Punic War**, Carthage was once again a prosperous merchant city, careful to avoid offending Rome. Certain Romans, however, maintained a lasting enmity toward the city-state. One public leader, **Marcus Porcius Cato** **(234-149 BC)**, declared again and again in the Roman Senate, "Delenda est Carthago!" (Carthage must be destroyed).

Cato touched a nerve, and circumstances in 149 BC led to the third and final Punic War. King **Masinissa** of Numidia began the conflict by provoking a war with Carthage on African soil. Needing to defend itself, Carthage organized its army to battle the Numidians. Responding to this "unauthorized" war, Rome demanded that Carthage hand over any and all of its war-making equipment: ships, weapons, etc. This was too much for the Carthaginians, who vowed never to give up their right to defend themselves.

The Carthaginians fought for three years against a deadly siege of their city. Ninety percent of the population of the city died from battle wounds or starvation. When the Romans finally overcame the last defenses, they found little worth preserving. The remaining Carthaginians were sold into slavery. The Romans pulled the walls and buildings of the city down and sowed the ground with salt to discourage anyone from building a city there again. Ironically, Rome itself would later build colonies of its own in North Africa, including one on the site of former Carthage.

The storming of the citadel of Byrsa, Carthage

10. GALLIC WARS
58-52 BC

In the history of warfare there have been few as effective and deadly as the Roman leader, **Julius Caesar (100-44 BC)**.

Caesar entered Cisalpine Gaul in 58 BC as a proconsul, sent to defend Rome's northern borders. The city-state of Rome retained a dread of the Gallic warriors who had sacked Rome in 390 BC, and Caesar was expected not only to protect, but perhaps to extend the border. Ever ambitious, Caesar intended far more than that; he envisioned a greatly expanded Roman empire, one that would stretch north through Gaul to reach the North Sea.

He was helped by two factors: Germanic aggression and Gallic division. The Germanic tribes located east of the Rhine River were constantly crossing the river to plunder Gallic territory, while the Gauls were divided into a number of bickering tribes that seldom cooperated. To justify his first encroachment on Gallic territory, Caesar used the excuse that he needed to repulse the advance of a Germanic tribe, the **Helvetti**, into Gaul. Caesar not only stopped the Helvetti, he also added large swaths of Gallic land to the Roman domain in the process. The Gauls protested, but they also valued the defense against the Germans, thus Caesar's aggression went unchecked.

From 57 to 54 BC, Caesar marched to the north to fight the fierce **Nervii** tribe in present-day Belgium. Continuing his drive to conquer, he built a fleet to cross what is now the English Channel to invade Britain. Any astute observer could see that Caesar was relentless in his desire for new lands and territories. To counter him, the Gauls finally came together under a new leader, **Vercingetorix**, chief of the **Arverni** tribe. United for the first time, the Gauls stopped Caesar at the fortress city of **Gergovia**, but then lost when they fought on the open plain. Retreating to **Alesia**, the Gauls were soon trapped in the city by 50,000 Roman soldiers, who built a siege wall. When the Romans discovered that a relief army of Gauls was on the march, they built an entire second set of walls outside the first and fought both armies from their fortified position within the two walls. Faced with the indomitable will of Caesar and the courage and discipline of his legions, Vercingetorix surrendered in 52 BC, ending the **Gallic Wars**.

Gallic Warriors

The remainder of the Romans' republican government seeped away during the last century before the birth of Christ. Landholding magnates developed huge estates in Italy, and veterans who returned from warfare in Africa or Greece found they could not afford a home of their own. Leaving their farms to join the urban poor in Rome, these men became dangerous to the state.

Largely in response to the urban problems of Rome and the agricultural crisis, three men came forward to serve as the unofficial rulers of the city: **Gaius Pompey (106-48 BC), Lucius Crassus, and Julius Caesar (100-44 BC).** When the **triumvirate** was formed around 60 BC, Pompey appeared to be the leader, but Caesar's glorious military success in the **Gallic Wars** (see no. 10) gave him enormous popularity in Rome. The third member, Crassus, had worked in banking and other services. Yearning for a military triumph of his own, Crassus took a Roman army into the Middle East and was defeated by the Parthians. As the decade drew to a close, the long-standing rivalry between Caesar and Pompey grew. Suspicious of Caesar's growing influence, Pompey led a movement in the Roman Senate that demanded Caesar surrender his command and come to Rome as a private citizen, without the protection of his legions.

Caesar decided to stay with his strength. He marched south across the **Rubicon River** into Italy on January 11, 49 BC, and his

Julius Caesar

legions came with him. Ever since, "crossing the Rubicon" has meant measuring one's chances, and then forging ahead.

Escaping from Rome as Caesar advanced, Pompey sailed east across the Adriatic Sea to Greece, while his sons (noted warriors themselves) sailed to Spain to stir up trouble for Caesar in that Roman province. This division of Pompey's forces gave Caesar a considerable advantage. Using the capital city of Rome as his bastion and forum, Caesar had Pompey and his followers named as enemies of the Roman Republic. Sending some of his best lieutenants to Spain to engage the sons, Caesar crossed the Adriatic Sea to play hide and seek with Pompey.

Although he had 50,000 men to Caesar's 30,000, Pompey was leery of an outright contest. He cleverly outmaneuvered Caesar, cutting off his supply lines. Caesar finally managed to provoke a battle at **Pharsalia** in Thessaly. Caesar won an overwhelming victory, and Pompey fled to Egypt where he was later assassinated by the Ptolemaic monarchy. Caesar himself traveled to Egypt, where he met the queen, **Cleopatra (69-30 BC).** Upon his return to Rome, Caesar's power was at its height. Frightened that Caesar would make himself a king, Roman consul **Marcus Junius Brutus (85-42 BC)** and others murdered him on the steps of the Roman Senate on March 15, 45 BC.

It came as little surprise to most Romans when the death of **Julius Caesar (100-44 BC)** failed to bring back the old Republic of Rome. The city-state and its empire were, by then, far too accustomed to military rule. Rome soon fell under the control of three men who formed the **Second Triumvirate: Marc Antony (82-30 BC), Gaius Octavian (63 BC-14 AD),** later known as **Augustus**, and **Lepidus**. Antony had been one of Julius Caesar's most trusted lieutenants; now he became leader of the legions as well as the lover of **Cleopatra (69-30 BC)**, queen of Egypt. Octavian was Caesar's nephew by adoption and his heir; he therefore inherited the immense fortune Caesar had acquired through years of warfare. Lepidus was a respected civil servant who was brought in to balance what was expected to be a fierce rivalry between Antony and Octavian. To simplify governance, the three men divided the Roman Empire into three administrative units; Octavian held control in the western section of the Mediterranean, Lepidus in the central area, and Antony in the eastern Mediterranean.

Allied with Cleopatra, Antony conducted campaigns in the east against the **Parthian Empire** in present-day Iraq. Failing to win any significant victories, he soon felt diminished by Octavian's success-

Caesar Augustus (Octavian)

es as an administrator. Running events in Rome, Octavian was able to sway public opinion; he made the most of Antony's failed efforts and hinted, through his extensive propaganda machine, that the interests of Egypt had become more important to Antony than those of Rome. Working together for once, Octavian and Antony deposed Lepidus from his position in 36 BC, after Lepidus brought his army from North Africa into Sicily.

With no middle-man, war broke out between Octavian and Antony in 32 BC. Using the tactics Julius Caesar employed with Pompey (see no. 11), Octavian had the Roman Senate declare Antony an enemy of the state. Gathering up a large army, Octavian sailed to the west coast of Greece to confront Antony and Cleopatra. The Egyptian queen had brought galleys and ships from her country in support, which resulted in a hard-fought contest between two giant naval forces. Octavian's fleet won the day, and Antony, despondent, fled to Egypt. Octavian pursued the lovers to Egypt; both Antony and Cleopatra committed suicide rather than be brought back to Rome as a spectacle. Octavian's victory ensured that Rome would be the central power of the Mediterranean for centuries to come.

13. ROMAN-GERMANIC WARS
16 BC-16 AD

The fierce warlike tribes who lived in present-day Germany were friendly neither to the Romans nor to the Gauls; **Julius Caesar (100-44 BC)** had cited German incursion across the Rhone River as an excuse to occupy Gaulish territory (see no. 10). Caesar pursued the **Helvetti** tribe to the banks of the Rhone and there fought a great battle in which the Germans, for all their courage and strength, were completely outmatched by the skill and professionalism of the Roman legions. In 57 BC, Caesar defeated the Germanic chieftain **Ariovistus**, who wanted to establish a base for his people on the western side of the Rhone. Later Caesar built a bridge across the **Rhine** River, near the present-day site of **Bonn**. Caesar's men inflicted great punishment on the German tribes across the bridge before turning back and destroying the bridge behind them.

During the reign of Caesar's nephew **Gaius Octavian (63 BC - 14 AD)**, Rome moved legions north and east of the Rhine border that Caesar had established. Invading German tribesmen crossed the Rhine and defeated Roman forces in 16 BC, but were soon subjected to punitive attacks by Octavian's stepsons, **Tiberius** and **Drusus**. Drusus stopped a German invasion of Gaul in 12 BC and won a major battle at the **Lippe River** against much larger Germanic forces. He then marched from the Rhine to the Elbe River to demonstrate Rome's command of the region. When Drusus died from injuries sustained when he fell from his horse, Tiberius carried out further attacks against the Germans.

In 4 AD, Tiberius returned to Germany and led naval and land forces to the Elbe River. Satisfied that things were in hand, he left Consul **Varro** in command and returned to Rome. In 9 AD a large Roman force of three legions, led by Varro, was ambushed by great numbers of Germans in the **Teutoburger forest**. The legions were annihilated, and Rome pulled back into a defensive posture along the Rhine River, a position it would maintain for roughly 300 years. Tiberius and **Germanicus Caesar** led punitive attacks against the Germans, but the front had stabilized at the Rhine River by 16 AD.

Octavian's stepson, Drusus

Judea had always been one of the most restive provinces of the Roman Empire, and in 66 AD, this residual discontent burst forth into a savage war that would bring down the last remnants of Jewish self-government. The causes of the rebellion were straightforward--in 62 AD, Rome deprived the Jews of certain citizenship rights, and Roman soldiers looted the city of **Jerusalem** in 66 AD.

The holy city was then taken over by a group of extremist Jews, known as the **Zealots**, who drove the Roman garrison from Jerusalem with heavy losses. The Jews rose in rebellion throughout the province and by the end of the year, most of Judea had fallen away from Roman control.

Emperor **Nero** of Rome sent an unknown senator, **Titus Flavius Vespasianus**, also known as **Vespasian (9-79)**, to quell the revolt. He entered **Galilee** with an army of 60,000 troops. Vespasian laid siege to the fortress of **Jotapa**, which was defended by **Flavius Josephus** (born Joseph ben Matthias). Josephus surrendered early in 68 AD after a 47-day siege and became a willing prisoner; he later wrote *The Jewish War*. Vespasian then marched south, subduing one town after another. Although the Jews lacked the weaponry and martial skill of the Romans, they fought with a ferocity that made even the toughest legionnaires fear them. Vespasian began to besiege Jerusalem in July 68 AD, but when he heard that Emperor

Titus Flavius Vespasianus

Nero had died and Rome was in the midst of a civil war, he contented himself with a holding action. Vespasian left for Rome in December 69 AD. His son, **Titus Flavius Sabinus Vespasianus (39-81)** remained to execute the siege of Jerusalem.

Titus brought four Roman legions, 25,000 auxiliary troops, and a siege train of 340 catapults to the battle. The Jews defended their city with fury, and it was not until the spring of 70 AD that Titus was able to penetrate the northern suburb of **Bezetha**. The Romans then battled their way into the city. On August 29, the fortified Temple was set aflame and on September 5, the city fell completely into the hands of the Romans. Thousands of survivors were sold into captivity, and Josephus claimed in his history that 1,100,000 Jews died in the siege.

The last strain of Jewish resisters held out at the fortress of **Masada** against repeated Roman attacks during 72 to 73 AD. When it became apparent the fortress would fall, **Eleazar ben Yair** and over 900 men, women and children killed themselves rather than surrender. Titus erected a huge arch in Rome to celebrate his victory, but the truth was far less triumphant--the Romans had pacified Judea at the price of thousands of Roman lives.

WARS OF ATTILA THE HUN
433-454 AD

When **Attila (406-453)** and his brother **Bleda** jointly inherited the kingship of the Huns in 433 AD, they started a series of wars that would make "Attila" and "Hun" synonymous with death and destruction. The Huns were a nomadic people from central Asia who spoke a language from the Ural-Altaic family. They crossed the Don River into southern Russia in 370 AD and soon pushed the **Visigothic** tribes south toward **Constantinople** and the **Ostrogothic** tribes west toward Roman **Gaul**. By the time that leadership passed to Attila and Bleda, the Huns had become tribally unified and possessed a large swath of land centered on the **Danube River** in eastern Europe.

Though they already received 700 pounds of gold yearly in tribute from Constantinople, Attila decided to terrorize the decaying Roman Empire further. He led a series of campaigns against the eastern half of the empire, centered on Constantinople, between 441 and 447. In 441, he devastated the Balkan provinces and in 477 went as far as the walls of Constantinople itself. The two rings of walls defending the city dampened Attila's zest, but he didn't leave until the

Atilla in Battle with Visigoths

Byzantines agreed to a treaty that increased the tribute to 2,100 pounds of gold a year.

After having his brother killed, Attila had complete control of the most dangerous marauding army ever seen in Europe. While he collected his indemnities from the eastern Roman empire, he cast an ambitious eye to the west. In 451, he led his hard-riding horsemen on a campaign that reached as far as Gaul, where the Huns plundered **Metz** and cities in present-day Belgium. He then charged south toward the city of Orleans and was met at **Chalons-sur-Marne** by an army composed of Roman legions and Visigothic tribesmen under Roman general **Aetius** and tribal leader **Theodoric**. The combined army of Romans and Visigoths managed to withstand the ferocious assaults of the Huns that day, and Attila, who had never been stopped in battle before, withdrew across the Rhine River.

In 452, Attila and the Huns moved south, across the Alps into northern Italy. They sacked the town of **Aquilea** so thoroughly that the survivors wandered southwest and soon founded a new town, which would become **Venice**. Vowing that he intended to win the Roman emperor's sister **Honoria** as his bride, Attila planned to attack Rome itself. He was visited, however, along the banks of the Mincius River in northern Italy by **Pope Leo I**, **The Great**, who apparently was very persuasive, because the Huns broke camp and rode north, over the Alps and out of Italy, never to return.

Attila died the following year. The most colorful reason given for his demise is that he burst a blood vessel on the night of his wedding to Hilda, a Gothic maiden. At any rate, with Attila's death, the threat from the Huns diminished, and within a century, they had been absorbed by the peoples around them in the Danube region.

Born in the merchant town of **Mecca**, near the west coast of the Arabian peninsula, **Mohammed (570-632)** showed little sign that his would turn out to be an astonishing life. Around the age of 40, he began to hear the voice of the archangel **Gabriel**, instructing him to listen to the word of **Allah** (God) and then to "Recite!" Mohammed gradually built a theology that was later enshrined in the writings of the **Koran**, the Muslim Bible.

Inspired by the voices that he heard to promote a relentless and uncompromising monotheism, Mohammed preached, "There is no God but Allah, and Mohammed is his Prophet." He was scorned in Mecca, and in 623 he retreated to the merchant town of **Medina**, 120 miles to the north, where he found a more willing audience. He soon became a desert warrior in the best traditions of the **Bedouin** tribesmen, preying on merchant caravans headed for Mecca.

The Prophet Mohammed

Mohammed's raids soon led to counter-raids by the **Koriesh** tribe from Mecca, led by able warrior **Abu Sufyan**. The first major battle came at **Badr** in January 624. Mohammed and his men defeated the Koriesh, demonstrating that Mohammed's message was intended to spread throughout Arabia. The Koriesh struck back, defeating Mohammed in the **Battle of Uhud** on March 23, 625. During the fight Mohammed was hit in the face by a stone, and the idea that he might perish led to panic among his men. The Muslims lost many men, but the Koriesh did not pursue.

Abu Sufyan came north again in 626 and laid siege to Medina; he was blocked and frustrated by a dry moat, and when he called off the siege and returned to Mecca, Mohammed proclaimed it as a great victory. In March 628, the Muslims and Koriesh agreed to the **Treaty of Hubaybiyah**, which declared there would be no war for ten years, and that Muslims could visit Mecca for pilgrimage on three special days of each year.

Mohammed turned north and campaigned to conquer the Jewish settlements at **Khaybar**. One of his subordinates went too close to the border of the Byzantine Empire and was defeated in the campaign of **Mu'tah** in 629. Mohammed himself wanted to march south, because the Koriesh had broken the terms of the treaty. By this time he had enough men and a fearsome reputation, that the Koriesh yielded the city without a fight. Mohammed and his followers entered Mecca on March 11, 630, and the Prophet removed all the idols from the sacred **Kabah**, a black meteorite that was worshipped by the people of Mecca. Mohammed led one last campaign, besieging the mountain city of **al Ta'if**, capital of the **Thaqif** tribe. Failing to capture the city, he obtained almost as much through negotiation as he would have from a conquest. Returning to Mecca, Mohammed had the satisfaction of knowing that most of Arabia (present-day Saudi Arabia) had been won over to the words of Gabriel and Allah.

The Seal of Mohammed

Some movements die with their leaders, while others live on because their leader had imbued them with fortitude. The latter was certainly the case with **Mohammed (570-632)** and the cause of **Islam**. At the time of the Prophet's death on June 8, 632, most of the Arabian peninsula was under the control of the new Islamic faith, but there had been little expansion into the larger world.

After Muhammad's death, the Arabs undertook campaigns against the **Persian Empire**, centered in present-day Iraq. The Arabs were in luck, since the Persians had been fighting for years against the **Byzantine Empire**, centered in Constantinople. Mohammed's successors managed to wrest **Syria** and **Palestine** from the Byzantines, and then turned their attention to the Persians. The Persians won the **Battle of the Bridge** on the Euphrates River in 634, and the Arabs countered by winning the **Battle of Buwayb** the following year.

The decisive battle against the Persians came in 641, at **Nahavand**. Following a prearranged plan, Arab horsemen fled from the field, drawing thousands of Persians in pursuit. The Arabs then regrouped and caught the Persians between two narrow mountain passes. Some chroniclers say as many as 100,000 Persians lost their lives in the battle. The last Sassanid Persian king was murdered in 651 and the Arabs soon took possession of all the Persian lands stretching from present-day Iraq to the borders with India.

The Arabs then turned again to the Byzantine Empire. They besieged Constantinople itself in 717 to 718, but were thwarted by the Byzantine fleet and its use of **"Greek fire"**, in which opposing ships were blasted with a sticky substance and then set aflame.

The horse warriors of Islam continued to expand as the eighth century opened. In 711, **Tarik ibn Ziyad** led a mixed force of Arabs and **Berbers** (from present-day Morocco) across what was called the **Pillars of Hercules**, the narrow body of water separating North Africa from the southern tip of Spain. Tarik's invasion met with success, and later generations of Spaniards bequeathed his name to the crossing point; **Gibraltar** was as close as the Spaniards could come to a pronunciation of the Arabic words "jebel Tariq" or Tarik's Mountain.

The Arabs and Berbers fought against the Visigothic kingdom of Spain, which had been created three centuries earlier, in the aftermath of the Roman Empire. Tarik's men won the crucial **Battle of Laguna de Janda** in July 711; Roderick, the last Visigothic king, was killed in the battle. The Arabs and Berbers moved rapidly northward. By 718, the Arabs and Berbers had taken over virtually all of Spain, and the last Christian holdouts had escaped to areas near the Pyrenees Mountains, where they established the Kingdom of **Navarre**.

By seizing the lands that had belonged to his brother Carloman, **Charlemagne** (shar-le-mane) **(742-814)** initiated a series of wars that would last his entire lifetime and preserve his name in European history. Charlemagne was instructed by his father, **Pepin the Great**, to share the Frankish kingdom equally with Carloman. Following his brother's death, Charlemagne became the sole King of the Franks.

Almost immediately, he mounted his first campaign outside of Frankland, invading **Lombardy** in northern Italy. In 772 he began what would become a deadly series of wars against the pagan Saxons of northern Germany. These wars, which raged off and on again until 804, were undertaken to convert the heathen. To the Saxons, they were simply acts of naked aggression.

Charlemagne then turned his attention to Muslim Spain. He marched south of the Pyrenees Mountains in 778 but was unable to penetrate the Muslim defenses. On his return, he offended the Christian Basques of Navarre. They attacked and destroyed Charlemagne's rear guard, which was led by his nephew **Roland**, at **Roncesvalles** on August 15, 778; that battle was later commemorated in poetry and song as **Le Chanson de Roland** (The Song of Roland). Charlemagne established a set of forts along the border and did not venture into Spain again.

The Franks were more successful in central and eastern Europe. Charlemagne invaded Lombardy a second time in 780 and made his son king of the Lombards. He undertook a punitive war against Brittany in 786 and conquered Bavaria in 787 to 788. He then turned his attention to the Avars, a warlike tribe located in the Danube region, who were believed by the Franks to be a second coming of the Huns. Charlemagne completely eliminated the **Avar** nation between 791 and 796;

using the tremendous treasury from his fallen foes, he began building a beautiful capital at **Aachen**.

On Christmas Day, 800 AD, Charlemagne was crowned Emperor of the Romans by **Pope Leo** in Rome. Wanting very much to recreate the Roman Empire of old, Charlemagne defeated the Saxons in 804, subdued the Bohemians in 805, and crushed the Danes and their Saxon allies from 808 to 810. In 811 he made his will, certain that the empire he had created would last as long as the original Roman Empire. He would have been saddened to know that his empire was quite defenseless against the marauders and pillagers who would come after his death: Viking, Magyar and Muslim raiders would bring death and destruction to nearly all parts of the former Carolingian empire.

Charlemagne crossing the Alps

25

Rollo near the mouth of the Seine River

Known as the **Vikings**, large groups of Scandinavian warriors from present-day **Norway, Sweden and Denmark**, they carried out raids and invasions of Europe for over 200 years. In the process, the Vikings brought cultural and material changes to a Europe that was nearly destroyed by the strength of their assaults.

The Holy Roman Empire of **Charlemagne** (see no. 18) was intended to last forever. Charlemagne's Frankish warriors were indeed able to ward off most threats by land. By water they were often outmaneuvered and defeated by the warriors from Scandinavia, who navigated up the long rivers of France and the Low Countries (the Netherlands, Belgium and Luxembourg). In their **long-boats**, ships with shallow drafts, they were able to operate in both the open sea and small rivers. Their ability to move quickly and the ferocity with which their warriors fought, allowed the Vikings to wreak havoc in Europe and the British Isles.

The first Viking raids were directed against Ireland in 795. The **Celtic** form of Christianity that had flourished for 400 years with little contact with Rome was severely damaged by the Viking raids, aimed at the wealth of the monasteries. The Vikings also struck against England and northern France, starting in the ninth century; soon, successful summer raids turned into year-long forays. The Vikings found it more profitable to maintain a permanent settlement on the coast of England or France, using it as the home base for each year's raids.

In 911, **Charles the Simple**, king of France, made a novel suggestion to **Rollo**, a Viking who had set up camp near the mouth of the Seine River. If Rollo would become a Christian, and marry one of the king's daughters, then he and his men could hold forever the land they presently occupied. Rollo agreed and his men, known to the French as "Northmen," soon carved out the province since known as **Normandy**.

Viking raids began to peter out in France, but they were approaching their height in England. A Danish monarchy was briefly created in England; King **Canute** was the most famous of the Scandinavian rulers. Ireland continued to be plagued by Viking invaders until 1014 when **Brian Boru** won the **Battle of Clontarf** and finally ended the menace to the Emerald Isle. The Vikings made their most progressive accomplishments far afield from Europe. **Leif Ericsson** and a handful of Vikings made the first known voyage to the New World around 1000 AD and set up a temporary settlement, probably in present-day Newfoundland. Swedish Vikings penetrated the rivers of Russia and founded a state centered on **Kiev**, in the present-day Ukraine. More than marauders, the Vikings brought the world navigational skills and demonstrated the advantages of a trade-based economy.

20. MAGYAR INVASIONS OF EUROPE
895-955 AD

Like the Huns who had pillaged in Europe during the fifth century, the **Magyars** were tribes of horse warriors from Central Asia. No one knows their exact origins, but it's certain that they made their first appearance on the European stage in 895 AD. Entering the Crimean peninsula of present-day Russia, the Magyars circled the southern edge of the Black Sea and found an area most conducive to their pastoral lifestyle: the **Great Hungarian Plain**, located between the Carpathian Mountains and the Danube River.

Once settled in, the Magyars began a series of devastating raids against Frankish domains to the west. By 900, the seven Magyar tribes had come together under the leadership of **Arpad**. The Magyars sent raiding parties against the **Byzantine Empire** in Constantinople, but the fortified walls of that city were too much for them. Concentrating instead on attacks into present-day Germany, the Magyars sent 33 raiding parties between 898 to 955. The German provinces of Saxony, Thuringia and Bavaria suffered the most from the Magyar invasions, and the Magyars became as dreaded to the people of Central Europe, as the Vikings were to the people along the coast.

The Germans earned a respite during the reign of King **Henry I, Duke of Saxony**. Known as "The Fowler," Henry stopped a major Magyar raid at **Riade** in 933 and then imposed a peace treaty. The treaty was broken by the Germans, and the Magyars resumed their raids into Germany and into present-day France from 951 to 954, and Italy. They ran

into a more unified German resistance at the **Battle of Lechfeld** (near present-day Vienna) in 955; **Otto I**, son of King Henry, defeated the Magyars in a great battle and sent the remainder of their force fleeing back to the Great Hungarian Plain.

Missionaries arrived from the Byzantine Empire, and by around 1000 AD, the Magyars had evolved into the Christian kingdom of Hungary. For hundreds of years thereafter, they would be considered some of the most stalwart defenders of the Christian faith in Europe. Even as they blended into Christian Europe in terms of faith, the Magyars retained a distinct cultural imprint from their earlier days as nomadic warriors; their language is part of the Finno-Ugric linguistic group, with twentieth-century Hungarian closer to Korean than to any modern European language.

Arpad, Magyar Leader

The **Arab-Berbers** (later called the **Moors**) conquered Spain (see no. 17), and set up a Muslim state meant to echo the grandeur of Baghdad, Damascus, Cairo, and Alexandria. Though the Moorish kingdom would in the end fall to a Christian reconquest, the effort would take hundreds of years of sacrifice and warfare.

In 912, the Muslim emir of Spain, **Abdar-Rahman III**, put down revolts by Arab dissidents and fought against the Christian kings of **Galicia** (northwest Spain) and **Navarre** (north-central Spain). Following his military successes, Abdar became the first caliph (both civil and religious leader) of Muslim Spain.

A second war, from 977 to 997, began after a power struggle ensued among the Muslim leaders in Spain. **Muhammad ibn-abi-Amir** invaded Galicia in 977, Leon in 988, and Castile in 989. By 997, the Moors controlled most of the Iberian peninsula (modern-day Spain and Portugal).

The third war lasted from 1001 to 1031, and involved a series of conflicts between the Muslim caliph, Arab and Christian dissidents, and an attempt by the Christian kingdoms in the north to damage the caliphate. The caliphate at Cordoba collapsed, and all pretense of a unified Muslim Spain began to break down.

A fourth war, from 1172 to 1212, began when Christian king **Alfonso VIII** of Castile campaigned against the Muslim Almohads who had invaded Moorish Spain. With the blessing of **Pope Innocent III**, Alfonso won a great victory at **Las Navas de Tolosa**. By the end of the fourth war, the Christian kingdom of Castile had firm control of central Spain.

The fifth war occurred from 1230 to 1248, and was launched by King **Ferdinand III** of Castile and Leon who launched a military crusade. He captured Cordoba in 1236 and Jaen in 1246. Seville, the capital of Andalusia, surrendered in 1248. Only the small kingdom of **Granada** in the extreme south of Spain remained to the Moors, and it was considered a vassal state of Castile. Following the war, the Christians ejected Moors from their homes for the first time in the Reconquista.

The sixth and final war, from 1481 to 1492, was led by King **Ferdinand V** and Queen **Isabella** of Aragon and Castile.

Ferdinand was defeated at Loja in 1482, but a Spanish fleet cut off provisions for the Moors from North Africa, and the Spaniards proceeded to capture Ronda in 1485, Loja in 1486, and Malaga in 1487. The culmination of the war, and of the entire Reconquista, came with the siege of Granada itself in April 1491 to January 2, 1492. When the city surrendered, Ferdinand and Isabella entered Granada on January 6, 1492, ending a 500-year process of reconquest.

The Moors surrender Seville to Ferdinand III

Most people in the English-speaking world can identify the importance of 1066 and the **Norman** conquest, but few know the extent of the Norman importance during the High Middle Ages. The Normans of 1066 were several generations removed from the **Viking** raiders who had settled Normandy in 911 (see no. 19). Devout Christians, ingenious castle builders and fierce fighters, the Normans combined the martial abilities of their Viking ancestors with Christian and Frankish allegiances. Despite their commitment to the Church, the Normans had a taste for battle and conquest.

An especially ambitious Norman, **Robert Guiscard (1015-1085)** and his Lombard princess **Sichelgaita**, landed in Arab-controlled **Sicily** in 1061 and started a war that would last for 30 years. The two eventually won control of the island for Guiscard and his brother, who would be crowned King **Roger I** of the Norman kingdom of Sicily. Even as they took land away from the Muslims, the Normans of Sicily found a new foe: the Byzantine Empire, which had long cherished dreams of incorporating Sicily and lower Italy.

During the first **Norman-Byzantine** war from 1081 to 1085, Guiscard sailed east and captured the island of **Corfu** and city of **Dyrrachium** from the Byzantines. After returning to Sicily, his warrior princess, Sichelgaita, who had often accompanied him in battle and was referred to as a true Valkyrie, remained prominent in the affairs of Sicily for the remaining five years of her life.

In the second Norman-Byzantine war from 1098 to 1108, Guiscard's son **Bohemund** rose to prominence. An important leader in the **Crusades** against the Muslims (see no. 23), Bohemund became prince of Antioch in 1099, where he renounced any tribute he might have owed to the Byzantine emperor, **Alexius I**. Bohemund was imprisoned by the

William the Conqueror

Arabs until 1103; upon his release he went to Europe and married the daughter of French King **Philip I**. Bolstered by this alliance, he launched a private crusade against the Byzantine Empire. Defeated in 1108, Bohemund became a vassal of the emperor.

No list of the Norman conquests would be complete without a reference to 1066. **Duke William of Normandy (1027-1087)**, also known as **William the Conqueror**, a great-great-great grandson of **Rollo** the Viking, claimed the English throne in 1066 and crossed the English Channel. At the landmark **Battle of Hastings** (October 14, 1066), he met and defeated the Anglo-Saxon army led by **Harold Godwinson** and was crowned King of England on Christmas Day, 1066.

Christian Europe suffered from overpopulation in the eleventh century; some scholars have speculated that this was the reason Europeans went to the Holy Land to fight.

The **Seljuk Turks**, a tribe of warriors originally from Central Asia, conquered the Middle East during the late eleventh century. The spectacle of the Holy City of **Jerusalem** in the hands of the Turks infuriated **Pope Urban II** who gave a rousing speech to thousands of French nobles at **Clermont** in 1095. Declaring that the Middle East was a land of "milk and honey," Urban urged the French knights to lead a crusade, a holy war, to reconquer the areas that had been lost by Christian pilgrims.

Leaders of the First Crusade

Before the knights could gear up for battle, an army of peasants (**the Peasants' Crusade**) marched east from France in 1095. Led by an itinerant preacher named **Peter the Hermit**, 30,000 poorly equipped men marched all the way to Constantinople, where they were greeted warily by the Byzantine emperor, **Alexius I Comnenus**, and his court. After being ferried across to Asia Minor (present-day Turkey), these first crusaders were ambushed in a mountain pass by the Turks. Although Peter the Hermit and some of his followers lived to tell the tale, many of the crusaders left their bones in Asia Minor.

The **Knights' Crusade** came a year later. Roughly 30,000 well-equipped members of the European nobility marched overland to Constantinople, where Alexius I Comnenus required them to swear fealty (faithfulness), as well as to promise they would recognize him as lord of any areas they might conquer. The knights then made their way through Asia Minor and besieged the ancient city of **Antioch**. After capturing the city, the crusaders were trapped inside by a huge army of Turks. Religious enthusiasm saved the day; a crusader came forward with a lance believed to be the **Holy Lance** that had pierced Christ's side as he lay on the cross. Fired with vigor at the sight, the crusaders left the safety of Antioch's walls and engaged the Turks in a battle won by the knights.

The crusaders then marched down the eastern coast of the Mediterranean and arrived at Jerusalem in June 1099. The crusaders discovered that the Turks had poisoned all of the wells within walking distance of the city, making an immediate conquest necessary. The crusaders purified themselves by marching around the city for three days with their heads bared. On a prearranged signal, they attacked, showing no mercy to whomever they met. Thousands of Turks, soldiers and civilians, were slaughtered.

Following the call of Pope Urban II, the knights had regained Jerusalem and the Holy Land. They soon divided the area into four separate Christian kingdoms and initiated a period of trade between the eastern and western parts of the Mediterranean.

Arab warriors entered **Jerusalem** in triumph, almost a century after the Crusader conquest (see no. 23). For the Muslims, the victory meant they had completed a **jihad**, or holy war, that had been declared in 1186.

Yusuf Salah ad-Din (1138-1193), known as the **Righteousness of the Faith**, and better known in the West by the name of **Saladin** (sal-a-deen), became vizier of Muslim Egypt in 1169. Saladin took his new post as a sign from Allah that he was destined to liberate Palestine from the grip of the crusaders. When his uncle, **Nur ad-Din**, died of a heart attack in 1174, Saladin became lord of both Syria and Egypt. What lay between his two domains was of course **Palestine**, called **Outremer** (land beyond the sea) by the crusaders.

The Crusader Kingdom of Jerusalem was led officially by King **Guy**, but one of his most important nobles, **Reynauld of Chatillon**, often took independent action. In 1181, Reynauld attacked a caravan of Arab pilgrims on their **haj** (pilgrimage) to **Mecca**. He later attacked **Medina** and tried to reach the holy city of Mecca, but was prevented by Saladin's brother, who sent Egyptian ships to stop the crusader forces.

Outraged by these actions, Saladin led his army from Syria into Palestine in 1183. The Arabs failed to capture any of the crusader cities and finally had to withdraw because of the need for Saladin's soldiers to plant their crops. This humiliating reverse inspired Reynauld to greater arrogance, and in 1186 he again assaulted a caravan of Arab pilgrims. This time Saladin called an official **jihad** and assembled troops from all over the Arab world in **Damascus** before he marched south against the Europeans.

Saladin entered Galilee on July 1, 1187, and lured the Christians away from Jerusalem. The crusaders marched in scorching heat and

A Templar Knight

arrived near Saladin's camp only to find that the Arabs had control of all the wells in the area. Due to the lack of water and the superior tactics of the Arabs, Saladin won a crushing victory on July 4, 1187 at the **Battle of the Horns of Hattin**. The Christian army was virtually destroyed.

Saladin had Reynauld brought to his tent, pulled out his scimitar, and beheaded Reynauld on the spot. Saladin joyfully witnessed the execution of all the prisoners who belonged to military orders such as the **Templar knights**. To his great credit, however, when he entered Jerusalem on October 2, 1187, he spared the population of the city. There was no wholesale massacre like the Christians had conducted in 1099; people were allowed to ransom their lives for a small amount of money. Saladin's jihad had succeeded, and Jerusalem would remain in Arab hands for exactly 780 years, to be lost in 1967 to the **Israeli Defense Forces** in the **Six Day War**.

Richard the Lion Hearted

By the end of the twelfth century, Jerusalem had fallen back into the hands of the Arabs, led by **Yusuf-Salah ad Din (1138-1193)**, also known as **Saladin** (see no. 24). In response, three prominent kings of Europe agreed to lead a crusade to once again gain possession of the Holy Land. King **Richard I, the Lion-Hearted (1157-1199)**, of England, King **Philip Augustus** of France, and **Henry Barbarossa**, Holy Roman Emperor, resolved to put aside their many differences and cooperate in a holy crusade.

Henry Barbarossa got off to a quick start. He led a large army of battle-hardened German warriors across eastern Europe, crossing from Constantinople into Asia Minor. However, after entering Turkey, Barbarossa drowned while going for a morning swim in the Seraph River. Disheartened by the loss of their leader, the Germans turned around and went home.

Richard and Philip came by sea. The moment they arrived in the Holy Land, they began to feud with one another. Although Richard was older and a more experienced warrior, he was technically the vassal of Philip. This strange circumstance had come about because of the Norman conquest of England (see no. 22) and Richard retaining his title as **Duke of Normandy**, making him a vassal of the King of France. Philip eventually pled illness and went home, where he immediately set about chipping away at Richard's territories in France.

Richard fought for months against Saladin and the Muslim warriors. In close combat, Richard's presence and military ability usually enabled the crusaders to win, but he could not manage what he wanted most: to gain entrance to Jerusalem. Indeed, Richard betrayed his own knightly principles when he ordered 2,600 Muslim prisoners to be killed because he could not find enough food to feed both them and his own men.

Eventually Richard and Saladin came to a temporary peace. The crusaders would leave the area, but would retain the coastal towns they still held, and Saladin agreed to allow Christian pilgrims to visit Jerusalem. Richard headed back to England, going this time by land. He was detained and then made a prisoner by the new Holy Roman Emperor, **Henry VI**, who demanded a large ransom for the English king. The people of London eventually raised 100,000 pounds of silver to pay for Richard's ransom, and he returned home. He planned actively for another crusade and also warred against King Philip in France. By the time of his death in 1199, King Richard the Lion-Hearted had spent only six months of his 10 years as king, in England proper.

26. CONQUESTS OF GENGHIS KHAN
1206-1227

More than any other individual in history, **Genghis Khan (1167-1227)** is associated with violent conquest. Beginning in 1206 when he was proclaimed as "great ruler" or "strong ruler" of the **Mongol** tribes, he carried warfare to all four corners of Asia. He was born with the name **Temujin** in the tent capital of **Karakorum**, in present-day Mongolia, and he rose rapidly to be named the Khan or supreme ruler by the great assembly of Mongols in 1206. At that time, he was around 40 years old, and his early years had taught him to be supremely ruthless; a quality he applied to virtually all the peoples he came across.

Genghis Khan's first major campaign was against the **Hsi Hsia Empire,** located in north-central **China**. He defeated the empire's soldiers and was acknowledged as overlord in 1209. In 1211, the Khan's soldiers went past the **Great Wall** of China and began a war against the **Chin Empire,** located in central and eastern China. Following an unsuccessful siege in 1214, Genghis Khan returned in 1215 and ruthlessly sacked **Peking,** the capital of the Chin empire.

In 1220, the Khan's emissaries to the ruler of the Kowarazeem kingdom in **Samarkand** were executed by **Shah Muhammad.** Enraged, Genghis Khan led his entire army (which many scholars believe never exceeded 120,000 men) westward and besieged Samarkand. The sack of that city was the most notorious of the Khan's many conquests of foreign cities. He pursued the heir of Shah Muhammad, **Prince Jalal ad-Din** northward into Russia, won a major battle against the Russia princes in 1223, and then returned to

Genghis Khan

Mongolia. He would not venture to Central Asia again.

A second war was fought with the Hsi Hsia empire from 1225 to 1227; this time the Khan was less magnanimous and the empire became thoroughly absorbed into the Mongol empire. Planning to conquer further in central and southern China, Genghis Khan died suddenly in 1227, somewhere south of Yinchuan, the present-day capital city of Hsi Hsia. At the time of his death, the Mongol realm stretched from the Pacific Ocean to the Black Sea, included northern China, and extended northward into the lower reaches of Siberia. To the west, it stretched all the way to the Volga plain in southern Russia.

The golden age of the troubadours of southern France, a time when poetry, chivalry and courtly love reigned, ended in blood and oppression as the result of a crusade called by **Pope Innocent III** against fellow Christians in 1208. The area of France that is today the province of **Languedoc** differed in language, culture, and religion from northern and central France. An extreme religious sect, the **Albigensians**, arose in that region toward the end of the twelfth century. The Albigensians believed that matter and spirit were irreconcilable, and that only the pure in heart and spirit could hope for salvation. Rejecting both the reality of Christ's death and the worth of the Catholic sacraments, the Albigensians presented a serious problem for the Catholic Church.

After the papal legate to the Albigensians was slain in 1208, Pope Innocent III proclaimed a full-scale crusade against the heretics of southern France. King **Philip II** of the **Capetian dynasty** in France declined to enter the fray, but he permitted his nobles to follow the Pope's instructions. Many nobles were happy to do so, since they wanted to acquire territory in southern France to add to their private domains.

Led by **Simon IV de Montfort**, the nobles of northern and central France won the **Battle of Muret** in September 1213. Count **Raymond VI** of Toulouse (the city at the center of the troubadour culture in Languedoc) undertook to protect the Albigensians. After withstanding a siege, his forces managed to reclaim all the land that had been lost to the invaders. A new king of France, **Louis VIII**, showed a stronger disposition to deal with the heretics than had his father; troops of the king marched south and captured most of Languedoc in 1226. The Albigensian heresy was suppressed, and many of the leaders committed suicide rather than surrender to the royal forces. The **Treaty of Meaux**, signed in 1229, brought the city and county of Toulouse under the rule of the Capetian dynasty, but the province of Languedoc retained its quasi-independence until 1271 when it was absorbed into the royal domain.

What had been called as a holy crusade to root out a heresy turned into a power struggle between the nobles of central and northern France against those of the south. The two major casualties of the war were the Albigensians and the joyous, spirited troubadour culture of Toulouse.

Persecution of the Albigensians

34

Beginning in 1223, the German order of **Teutonic Knights** began a series of wars intended to conquer and Christianize the areas of northeastern Europe where Germany, Poland and Lithuania are today. Though their mission became clouded by worldly ambitions, they left a rich legacy of castle-building and war-making.

Founded in 1198 as the Teutonic Knights, or the Order of the Germans of the Hospital of St. Mary, the knights were crusaders who had fought in the Holy Land. Migrating north, they were invited by the Polish duke of Masovia to settle along the Vistula river in northwestern **Poland**. Almost at once, the knights began a series of wars to conquer the area now known as Prussia and bring the Prussians to Christianity. The long **Teutonic-Prussian Wars** raged from 1223 to 1283 and ended in complete success for the knights. They were not as successful in their invasion of Russia, where they were stopped by Orthodox Christians led by **Alexander Nevsky (1220-1263)** at Lake Peipus in 1242.

The knights were led by a Grand Master, assisted by five grand lords, and they wore a uniform of a white coat with a black cross. Their fierce appearance and fighting style intimidated many potential foes, Christian and heathen alike. By the start of the fourteenth century, many Polish nobles began to wonder whether it was wise to allow such a formidable military force to remain within the bounds of the country, especially since the knights insisted on putting all the land they conquered under the rule of the Pope.

Fourteenth century Teutonic Knight leader

Poland made an alliance with **Lithuania** and in 1309 began to fight against the knights. The knights were defeated by the Poles at the **Battle of Plowce. The Treaty of Kalisz** in 1343 left the province of **Pomerelia** in the hands of the knights, while Poland reclaimed other lands it had lost. Pomerelia was crucial, however, because it was Poland's only access to the sea. Equally offensive to the Poles was the fact that the Knights' Grand Master had made Marienburg castle, near the Polish city of Danzig, into his new chief residence.

In 1410, the Grand Duke of Lithuania again joined with Poland to fight against the knights. Poland and Lithuania won a decisive victory at the **Battle of Tannenberg** in 1410; the Grand Master and most of his subordinate commanders were killed in the 10-hour battle. The ensuing **Treaty of Thorn** took the province of Samogita away from the knights and gave it to Lithuania. A final conflict between Poland and the knights, known as the **Thirteen Years' War**, took place from 1454 to 1466, and ended with the surrender of much of the knights' land to Poland; the knights accepted Polish sovereignty over their remaining holdings. Retaining East Prussia, they made their new capital at **Konigsberg**, and lasted as a military order until the early nineteenth century when they were dissolved by **Napoleon I**.

The death of **Genghis Khan (1167-1227)** did not stop the relentless stream of battles, wars, and conquests that he had begun. Genghis' successors during the thirteenth century, **Ogedi, Kuyuk, Mangu,** and **Kublai (1216-1294),** continued the Mongol policy of relentless expansion.

Two years after the death of Genghis, the Mongol tribe named his son Ogedi as his successor. Prone to bouts of both drunkenness and laziness, Ogedi nonetheless allowed his generals to initiate wars against the **Chin Empire** from 1231 to 1234, the **Sung Empire** in southern China, starting in 1236, and even eastern Europe. Mongol horsemen penetrated as far as Hungary in 1241 before they turned back due to Ogedi's death. The Mongols sudden return to Asia likely saved Europe from Mongol domination.

Kuyuk, a grandson of Genghis, became the next Khan in 1246. Initiating no new wars or policies, he ruled the Mongol empire for only two years before his death in 1248. **Mangu,** another grandson, was named as the next Khan in 1251. Under Mangu, the Mongols made a definite commitment to expansion and development in eastern Asia (China in particular), rather than in the Middle East or western Europe. Mangu's younger brother **Hulegu** was given command of the Mongol forces in Central Asia, which carried out a devastating war against the **Abbasid caliphate** from 1255 to 1260, that ended with a ferocious sack of **Baghdad,** but also a loss to the Mameluke soldiers of Egypt at the **Battle of Ain Jalut** in 1260. Mangu himself planned to conquer **Korea,** but he died of dysentery prior to the invasion.

Mangu was succeeded by another brother, Kublai, who became Khan on June 4, 1260. Probably the most intelligent of all the successors to Genghis, Kublai would become famous in Europe due to the travels and writings of **Marco Polo (1254-1324),** the Venetian trader, who lived for years at the Khan's court. During Kublai's long reign, Mongol armies succeeded in subduing the resilient **Chung dynasty** in southern China, ending a series of wars that had begun under Ogedi in 1236. The Khan's victorious troops then marched into southeast Asia for the first time. They encountered difficulties, fighting in a jungle terrain with which they were unfamiliar, against enemies who used elephants. The Mongols were defeated in their first invasion of the **Kingdom of Annam** which began in 1281 and ended in 1285, but a second onslaught in 1286 brought the king of Annam to pay tribute to Kublai. Marco Polo accompanied the Khan on his campaigns against the **Kingdom of Pagan** in modern-day Burma in 1283 and again in 1287, which ended with Pagan acknowledging the sovereignty of Kublai. Kublai's most costly--and well-known--failures came with his two invasions of the island of **Japan** in 1274 and in 1281. Both times, large Mongol armies carried by Korean ships were turned back by a combination of bad weather and Japanese resistance. Kublai Khan died in 1294. His single greatest achievement had been to unify all of China under one rule, and the **Yuan dynasty** he created held sway in that country until 1370.

Kublai Khan

The area now known as Switzerland began its long struggle for independence in 1291. Descendants of the **Helvetians**, a Celtic people who had been conquered by **Julius Caesar (100-44 BC)**, the Swiss were dominated by the **Habsburg** family, which ruled both **Austria** and the **Holy Roman Empire**. In 1291, upon hearing that Holy Roman Emperor **Rudolph (1218-1291)** had died, the leading citizens of the cantons of **Uri**, **Schwyz** (for which the country would later be named), and **Unterwalden** met on a tiny heath called **Rutli**, on the shores of Lake Lucerne. Declaring an **Everlasting League** (the long title was the Confederation of the League of Upper Germany), they swore to join together to preserve their political independence and cultural identity.

The Habsburgs were not willing to relinquish their claim to the areas north of the Alps, and so the burly Swiss mountaineers banded together to meet the Austrian army of **Duke Leopold III** at the **Battle of Morgarten** in 1315. The Swiss troops, fighting on foot, defeated the mounted Austrians.

Encouraged by this show of strength, five new cantons--Lucerne, Zurich, Bern, Zug, and Glarus--entered the league between 1322 and 1353. Bavarian troops tried to conquer the area in 1355, but they were turned back by the same combination of rugged terrain and smart military tactics that the Swiss had used so well against the Austrians.

The Austrians made another attempt to reconquer Switzerland in 1385. Leopold led the Austrian invasion that culminated in the **Battle of Sempach**. The heavily armored Austrian cavalry men dismounted to fight on foot against the more mobile Swiss, who overwhelmed them with halberds and pikes. Leopold and most of his knights perished in the battle, but Austria tried again in 1388, only to be defeated in the **Battle of Nafels.** Finally, in 1394, Austria signed a 20-year peace treaty and abandoned its claims to land in Lucerne, Zug and Glarus. Although it was still called a dependency of the Holy Roman Empire, Switzerland was in fact autonomous and self-governing.

The Battle of Sempach

Robert the Bruce and William Wallace

The long series of wars between England and Scotland, that gave independence to Scotland, began in 1295. The deaths of Scottish King **Alexander III** in 1286 and his granddaughter, **Margaret of Norway** in 1290, left the throne of Scotland open to the contentious factions led by **Robert the Bruce (1274-1329)** and **John Balliol**. This crisis in Scottish affairs provided an opening for English King **Edward I**, who proposed to mediate and conciliate between the two factions. Edward chose Balliol to be king in 1292 and then imposed a state of vassalage on both Balliol and the entire country of Scotland.

Balliol rebelled in 1295, and in 1296 he was deposed by Edward, who marched northward with English troops. Edward's forces captured most of the Scottish cities, stole the **Stone of Scone** (on which all Scottish kings had previously been crowned), and returned to England. He left behind three commissioners and a number of military garrisons to run the country and quell future uprisings.

A Scottish commoner, **William Wallace (1272-1305)**, came forward to lead a rebellion against English rule. Using unconventional military tactics, especially the deployment of massed pikemen, Wallace surprised and defeated a large English army at the **Battle of Stirling Bridge** in 1297. Alarmed, Edward again marched north, and his large force overwhelmed Wallace's army at the **Battle of Falkirk** in 1298. Wallace escaped from the battle to pursue deadly guerrilla warfare against the English garrisons. Edward went north again in 1303, defeated Wallace's troops on the open field, and then waited for Wallace to be betrayed. The Scottish patriot was tried, hung, drawn and quartered, but the memory of his courage and patriotism remained to inspire other Scots.

Robert the Bruce had played a double game during Wallace's revolt, but in 1306 he murdered his only serious rival for the throne and had himself crowned King of Scotland at Scone (without the benefit of the Stone, still in England). Edward I made one last campaign; he defeated Bruce and forced him to flee to Ireland. Edward's death in 1207 deprived England of its most effective military leader, and Bruce soon returned to Scotland to carry on a border war. He won the crucial **Battle of Bannockburn** in 1314 and repelled an invasion by English King **Edward II** in 1322. **The Peace of Northampton** of 1328 gave legal independence and sovereignty to Scotland. Scotland had gained its freedom, and although it would be joined with England in 1603, the northern section of the island would never consider itself merely another part of England; it was truly its own land, in culture, heritage and pride.

The Byzantine empire had withstood the attacks of many enemies, starting with **Attila the Hun (406-453)**, but in 1302 it encountered a foe it could not best: the **Ottoman Turks. Osman I (1259-1326)**, founder of the Ottoman empire, started the series of wars in 1302 with a victory over the Byzantines near the city of Nicomedia. The Byzantine city of **Bursa** fell to the Ottomans in 1326 and became the capital city of their new empire.

A second war broke out in 1329 to 1338, after the Ottomans settled on the **Gallipoli** peninsula. Using Gallipoli as a jumping-off point, the Ottomans entered Byzantine Europe, invaded Thrace and Macedonia, and captured Nicaea and Nicomedia in 1337. By 1338, the Ottomans had subdued all of Byzantine Europe.

The third war between the Byzantine and Ottoman empires began in 1359, when the Turks surrounded Constantinople on all sides. Byzantine Emperor **John V** went to Rome by ship and begged for help from the Papacy. Constantinople did not fall, but the Ottomans took the rest of Macedonia in 1371, and a Christian army composed of Serbs, Bulgars, Bosnians, Albanians and volunteers from as far away as France was completely defeated by the Turks at the crucial **Battle of Kosovo** in 1389. The Byzantine Empire knew it was on its own. It could expect no further help from Western Europe,

Muhammed II

which was in the throes of both the **Hundred Years' War** (see no. 33) between France and England and the division of the papacy between Rome and Avignon.

The fourth war lasted for one year in 1422. Byzantine emperor **John VIII** plotted to wrest the Ottoman throne from Sultan **Murad II**, but Murad crushed the effort and in retaliation, marched his army to assault Constantinople. He was eventually forced to withdraw, beaten by the thickness of the walls and the strength of the Byzantine fleet.

The final Turkish-Byzantine war (1453 to 1461), began when Sultan **Muhammad II**, "the Conqueror" again laid siege to Constantinople. Muhammad and his generals had specialized in the development of siege artillery, and they brought enormous cannons to the battle (one required fifty oxen to pull it and two hours to load). A seven weeks' siege ended on May 29, 1453, when the Ottoman army broke through the walls and entered the city. The last Byzantine emperor perished on the steps of a church. The loss of the city greatly disheartened Christian Europe, and from 1453 until the late 1600s, fear of "the Turks" was uppermost in the minds of many Europeans. The last Byzantine resistance was extinguished in 1461, when the Turks captured **Trebizond** on the Black Sea.

Joan of Arc

The long-standing rivalry between the French and the English began during the fourteenth century and hardly abated until the twentieth! During the High Middle Ages, both the English and French belonged to the Roman Catholic Church. Dynastic and commercial rivalries festered and gave rise to a war that lasted for over five generations.

The last of the Capetian kings of France died in 1337. King **Edward III (1312-1377)** of England claimed the throne of France, but the French nobles gave the title to **Philip of Valois**, which began the Valois dynasty. The two countries were also vying for commercial control of the area known as **Flanders**, present-day Belgium, where the wool trade was competitive and profitable. For these reasons, England and France went to war in 1340.

France had a population four to five times as large as England, and its knights had the longest and most distinguished military tradition in Europe. The English had two

strengths: control of the sea and the **longbow**. Controlling the English Channel meant that King Edward III could invade France at will, while the longbow neutralized the power of the French knights who had for so long dominated warfare in medieval Europe. A well-trained English longbowman could fire through the slits in a knight's armor from two hundred yards away. He could also shoot several arrows per minute. The **crossbow**, used by the French, took much longer to arm.

The major battles were won by the English: small English armies defeated much larger French ones at **Crecy** in 1346, **Poitiers** in 1356, and **Agincourt** in 1415. The English took possession of large areas of the French countryside, and after Agincourt, they actually held Paris itself for a number of years. The uncrowned French dauphin, **Charles VII (1403-1461)** retired to a truncated France, south of the Loire River. Things looked grim for France, until a peasant maid, seventeen years of age, emerged as the new champion of the Valois monarchy and the French people. An innkeeper's daughter, **Joan of Arc (1412-1431)** led French troops to victory at **Orleans** in 1429 and then escorted the dauphin to Rheims Cathedral, where he was crowned and anointed as the King of France. Joan was captured a year later by the Burgundians (a French faction that sided with England) and burned to death after being convicted of being a witch in a church court.

Her courage had unified the French, and given them new hope. Using a military innovation--the first cannons in Europe--the French slowly pushed the English out of Paris and northwest France. The last battles were fought in Normandy in 1453; when they were over, France had become truly French, and the two countries had developed an enmity that would endure for centuries.

Born near Kesh in Transoxiana (present-day Uzbekistan), **Timur (1336-1405)** was a Turk and a devout Muslim. He was wounded by an arrow early in life and was thereafter called **Timur-I Lang**, meaning Timur the Lame, which Europeans later converted to **Tamerlane**. From modest beginnings, he rose to become the supreme leader of the Turkish tribes in Transoxiana by 1369, and as a result, Islam reclaimed its influence in that region.

In 1375, Tamerlane began a series of campaigns that would make both Asia and Europe tremble in fear. He took control of the Khanate of the **Golden Horde** and then began to expand in a southwest direction from his capital at **Samarkand**. He invaded Khurasan (present-day Afghanistan) in 1381, and in 1388, turned northeast again and fought against his former protégé, **Tokhtamish**, ruler of the Golden Horde. Having subdued his rival, Tamerlane began what was called the **Five Years' Campaign** in which he fought in Iran, Iraq, Asia Minor and southern Russia from 1392 to 1397. Following his destruction of the Golden Horde, he demolished the Tartar cities of Astrakhan and New Sarai.

In 1398, Tamerlane turned his gaze southward toward India. In a brutal display of power, he massacred 50,000 prisoners and captured **Delhi**. The city was left in ruins, and Tamerlane returned to Samarkand, as he did after each successful campaign. The next

Tamerlane

year he began what was called the **Seven Years' Campaign** from 1399 to 1405, during which he marched on Georgia, Asia Minor and the ancient cities of the Middle East. **Aleppo** in 1400, and **Damascus** in 1401, opened their doors to him, and in 1401 he carried out a ferocious sack of the famed city of **Baghdad**. On July 20, 1403, he won an enormous victory over the Ottoman Turks at **Angora** in Asia Minor. No friend to Christian Europe either, Tamerlane captured **Smyrna** on the Black Sea from the **Knights of St. John**; only his preoccupation with the Middle East and Asia prevented him from undertaking a conquest of all of Europe.

Tamerlane returned in triumph to Samarkand in the summer of 1404. He departed from the city in November with an enormous army, intending to defeat and conquer the Ming emperor of China. Worn out from his many campaigns, Tamerlane died at Otrar in present-day Kazakhstan. The **Timrud dynasty** he founded lasted for a century after his death.

It was believed that if Tamerlane were ever raised above ground again, an even greater terror would appear. Russian Professor M.M. Gerasimov exhumed Tamerlane's body on June 22, 1941; he confirmed Tamerlane's lameness and determined his height was five feet eight inches. On that same day, Hitler's army invaded Russia, beginning a bloody war.

The enormously complicated **Wars of the Roses** began in 1455 for two reasons: the English population was angry over the conduct of the **Hundred Years' War** (see no. 33), and two ducal houses were competing for the English throne. The Hundred Years' War finally ended in 1453, and many English people were resentful over the high taxes they had paid to support a war that in the end had lost all English land in France.

To make matters worse, the **House of York** maintained that the **House of Lancaster's** King **Henry VI (1457-1509)** and his wife, **Margaret of Anjou**, sat on the throne by mistake. **Richard, Duke of York**, believed he had a superior claim to the throne since he was descended from the third son of King **Edward III**, while King Henry VI was descended from the fourth son of that monarch.

In 1450, Richard forced the king to recognize him as the heir to the throne. In 1453, King Henry VI went temporarily insane, and in that same year his wife bore a son, who obviously took precedence over the claim of the Duke of York. The king recovered from his illness in 1454, and Richard, finding himself excluded from the royal council, took up arms, starting the thirty-year-long Wars of the Roses between the House of Lancaster, which displayed a red rose as its emblem, and the House of York, with its white rose.

The House of York won the **Battle of St. Albans** in 1455, but in 1459 Richard and his

Henry VII

key supporters fled the country, then returned to win the **Battle of Northampton** in 1460, where King Henry VI was taken prisoner. Queen Margaret continued to fight, and her forces won the **Battle of Wakefield** in which Richard was killed. Richard's son Edward assumed leadership of the House of York, assisted by the **Earl of Warwick**.

The Yorkists won the **Battle of Towton** in 1461, and Edward was crowned as King Edward IV. Soon after the coronation, the Earl of Warwick changed sides, and by 1470 Warwick had forced the young king to seek refuge in Holland; Henry VI was restored as king. Edward returned from Holland and won the **Battle of Barnet** where Warwick was killed; Queen Margaret was defeated at the **Battle of Tewkesbury** in 1471, and imprisoned, Henry VI's son was killed, and King Henry VI died in the Tower of London.

In 1483, Edward IV died and was succeeded by his twelve-year-old son, **Edward V. Richard, Duke of Gloucester**, usurped the throne on June 26, 1483, and both the child-king and his younger brother were murdered, probably at Richard's command. King Richard III ruled the country for two years before he was defeated and killed at the **Battle of Bosworth Field. Henry Tudor, the Earl of Richmond**, who won the battle, took the throne as **Henry VII**, starting the Tudor line. He married a princess from the House of York, thereby ending the conflicts.

In the fifteenth century, a new power arose to contest the position of France and the Holy Roman Empire: the duchy of **Burgundy**. Originally a small dukedom within the kingdom of France, Burgundy came close to achieving substantial power, and was only brought down by the actions of a very small, but determined state to its south.

During the **Hundred Years' War** (see no. 33) between France and England, the dukes of Burgundy acquired a good deal of independence from their mother country. **Philip the Bold, John the Fearless, Philip the Good (1396-1467)**, and **Charles the Bold (1433-1477)** brought Burgundy commercial and political importance, and created a court life renowned for its opulence.

The reign of Duke Philip the Good brought the greatest expansion. Philip moved his court to **Brussels**, and expanded the boundaries of his dukedom to include Flanders, Brabant, Luxemburg, Limburg, Gelderland, Zeeland, Holland, Artois, and part of Picardy. There was some reality to the description of Burgundy as the "Middle Kingdom," lodged between France and the Holy Roman Empire; such a rich and powerful dukedom made its neighbors nervous.

The reign of Charles the Bold brought anxieties to a head. Flamboyant and ambitious, Charles seemed likely to continue Burgundy's policy of expansion. The Swiss made an alliance with unlikely partners, the **Habsburgs** in Austria and cities in southern

Charles the Bold

Germany, and started a war to assure its northern border. King **Louis XI** of France (known as the Spider King because of his adroit diplomacy), sent funds to help the Swiss in their fight with Burgundy.

The Swiss repelled the Burgundians at **Hericourt** and took some Burgundian land along the Swiss border. After Charles the Bold's troops killed the entire Swiss garrison at **Granson** in February 1476. The Swiss infantry routed the Burgundians at Granson on March 2 and at **Morat** on June 2. Charles himself joined in on January 5, 1477 at the **Battle of Nancy**. The Swiss encircled and defeated the Burgundians, and Charles was killed while trying to escape.

The Burgundian state fell apart in the wake of the defeats and Charles' death. Burgundy reverted to its earlier status as a French province, and the Burgundian possessions in northern Europe eventually formed into the **Netherlands** and **Belgium**. The Swiss confirmed their independence with the victory at Nancy, and two new cantons (Fribourg and Solothurn) asked to be admitted to the confederacy. Disputes arose, and Switzerland came close to civil war. Into the crisis stepped a hermit named **Nicholas von der Flue**. He made a dramatic appeal to the Swiss **Diet** (legislature), persuading his fellow Swiss to settle the matter through compromise rather than warfare. The two new cantons were admitted and Flue was recognized as the great mediator in the matter.

Many Spaniards followed in the path of **Christopher Columbus (1451-1506)**, determined to find gold and glory in the New World. Among the most remarkable of these conquistadores was **Hernando Cortez (1485-1547)**, who almost single-handedly brought down one of the world's greatest empires. Having arrived in **Hispaniola**, Cortez heard rumors of a powerful and wealthy Indian civilization, located well inland from what is now known as the east coast of **Mexico**. In 1520, he landed on the coast with roughly 600 Spanish soldiers, horses and cannon. It was quite a tiny force with which to challenge the **Aztec Empire**, which had arisen around 1300 and subjugated most of the other Indian peoples in central Mexico. Nevertheless, Cortez and his men began the long, uphill march toward **Tenochtitlan** (present-day Mexico City), the Aztec capital.

Cortez was either prescient or extremely lucky, because he approached Tenochtitlan at a low moment for the Aztec monarch, **Montezuma II (1480-1520)**. The Aztecs believed that a god named **Quetzacoatl** would come from the east, and the first information Montezuma received indicated that Cortez and the Spaniards might be that God, since Cortez arrived with dogs and horses (animals unknown in the Western hemisphere), and cannon that belched smoke and destruction. Montezuma sent messengers asking Cortez to stay away from the city, offering him gifts of gold and silver. These gifts served to embolden the Spaniards, and they eventually reached Tenochtitlan. As they came into view of the city, the Spaniards were amazed by the architecture, especially the many interlocking canals that wove around the city. This vision of beauty and development would not survive the war.

Welcomed by Montezuma, Cortez soon took the Aztec emperor hostage to guarantee the safety of his men. Learning that the city was ready to rise up against him, Cortez and his men fought their way out in what the Spanish called "Noche Triste" (Night of Sorrows). Cortez gained Spanish reinforcements along the coast and recruited numerous Indian allies, who were tired of Aztec rule. Returning to Tenochtitlan, he and his men laid siege to the city and fought a series of deadly battles to win control of the capital and surrounding area. By 1522, Cortez had achieved complete control. The price was overwhelming for the Aztecs, who had lost 150,000 people.

Hernando Cortez

Martin Luther's (1483-1546) protest against the corruption of the Roman Catholic Church in 1517 had led to the development of several other faiths: Lutheranism, Calvinism, Anabaptism, and others. In France, the king and his court remained staunchly Catholic, as did the large majority of the population. About 10 percent, became **Huguenots**, followers of **John Calvin (1509-1564)** and his religious doctrines.

For centuries, France had followed the doctrine of "one king, one law, one religion." After 1550, the country found itself deeply divided between Catholics and Huguenots. Other countries did not stay meekly on the sidelines. Catholic Spain sent assistance to the French Catholic majority, while England and the Netherlands sought to aid the Huguenot minority.

The fighting began in 1562. One of the most violent episodes occurred 10 years later, when King **Charles IX** summoned thousands of Huguenots to Paris to celebrate the wedding of the king's sister to **Henry IV** of Navarre **(1553-1610)**, a leading Huguenot from the south of France. Charles probably meant well at first, but he was mentally unstable and heavily influenced by his mother, **Catherine de Medici.** Listening to the advice of his mother and others, the king ordered a massacre of the Huguenots within the city. The **St. Bartholomew's Day** massacre was imitated in other French cities; at least 20,000 Huguenots lost their lives within a few terrible weeks.

The Queen Mother and her advisors had been mistaken to believe terror would dissuade the Huguenots, who instead fought

John Calvin

back more fiercely than ever. Henry of Navarre slowly became the focal point, and in the 1580s, the country dissolved into the War of the three Henrys, fought between King **Henry III** (who had succeeded Charles IX), **Henry the Duke of Guise**, and Henry of Navarre. After King Henry III was stabbed and killed by a madman in 1593, the French people were so weary of war and tumult that Henry of Navarre was asked if he would convert to Catholicism in order to gain the throne. Saying that "Paris is worth a mass," Henry of Navarre was crowned King Henry IV in 1594, ending the wars of religion in France. In 1598 he issued the **Edict of Nantes**, which asserted that Catholicism was the religion of the majority of Frenchmen.

45

EIGHTY YEARS' WAR
1568-1648

What is presently called Holland is actually the **United Provinces of the Netherlands**, an area that won its freedom from Spain during the sixteenth and seventeenth centuries. Famed for their artistic and commercial skill, the Dutch were among the first in Europe to win freedom from an oppressive power and experiment with an oligarchy responsive to the wishes of the people.

Charles V (1500-1558), King of Spain and Holy Roman Emperor, was actually Flemish by birth. A series of fortunate dynastic events had brought to him the crowns of Spain, Germany, and his native land. In addition, Charles ruled Spain from 1520 to 1556, during the years in which **Hernando Cortez (1485-1547), Francisco Pizarro (1470-1541)** and other conquistadores vastly expanded Spanish claims in the New World. Charles abdicated the throne in 1556, giving his vast possessions to his son, **Philip II (1527-1598)**. Having been raised in Spain, Philip was not as sensitive to his Flemish and Dutch subjects as his father had been, and in 1568 several provinces of the Netherlands broke out in revolt. The freedom-loving Dutch were largely Calvinist, and Philip had tried to force Catholicism upon them.

Philip sent thousands of Spanish soldiers north to conquer the Netherlands, under the leadership of the **Duke of Alva** and **Duke of Parma**. Both were skillful soldiers and the

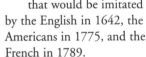

The Duke of Alva

Spanish were the best infantrymen of their day, but they were fighting against a people desperate to save their homeland and freedom. The Dutch were willing to break holes in their dikes and flood large sections of the countryside rather than lose those areas to the Spanish.

In 1581, the top Dutch politicians and merchants solemnly "abjured" Philip II as their monarch, citing his abuses against their people.

Declaring the seven United Provinces of the Netherlands free and sovereign, the Dutch started a revolutionary tradition that would be imitated by the English in 1642, the Americans in 1775, and the French in 1789.

Unable to prevent Protestant England from helping the Dutch rebels, Philip II sent the **Spanish Armada** against England in 1588. When that effort failed, Philip's ability to quell the Dutch revolt began to fade. Spain fought on until 1609, when a truce was agreed to. When the **Thirty Years' War** (see no. 41) began nine years later, Spain and the Netherlands again went to war. By then, the Dutch had become masterful seamen, and they preyed upon Spanish shipping both in Europe and the Caribbean. When the Thirty Years' War came to an end in 1648, Spain agreed to the full and complete independence of the Netherlands, 80 years after the conflict had begun.

King **Philip II (1527-1598)** of Spain and Queen **Elizabeth I (1533-1603)** of England were mortal enemies, each sworn to uphold their different faiths (Catholic and Anglican), and each ambitious for the welfare of their different countries. The two monarchs contended for position for years before they came to blows over Spanish treasure and possessions in the New World.

Elizabeth had long ignored English privateers who preyed on Spanish shipping in the **Caribbean**, but in 1580 she actually licensed Captain **Francis Drake (1540-1596)** to harass the Spanish anywhere in their New World territories. Taking his queen at her word, Drake attacked **Panama**, then sailed south, completely around South America, and appeared on the west coast of that continent where he took the Spanish colonists completely by surprise. Drake pillaged and burned Spanish South America and sailed north to present-day California, before he turned west across the Pacific Ocean. Arriving in London in 1582, after only the second circumnavigation of the globe (the first had been accomplished by Ferdinand Magellan), Drake was knighted by Queen Elizabeth for his exploits. Drake became the model for the new Elizabethan Navy that was under development to defend against a possible Spanish invasion.

Furious over the incursions into his territories, Philip II slowly assembled a massive fleet of 130 ships that has become known as the **Spanish Armada**. Sailing north from Spain in 1588, the Armada ran into fierce English resistance. The lightly armed and more maneuverable English ships inflicted considerable damage, although it was a combination of the use of fire ships and a storm that truly defeated the Spanish. Only half of the ships returned to Spain.

Far from giving up, Philip gathered similar fleets in 1593 and 1594, but bad weather and lack of supplies always prevented his sailors from reaching their objectives. Drake himself was killed in an abortive attack on a South American city, and the war began to peter out after Philip's death in 1598.

An acute rivalry had built up between the two countries. Many English subjects were disappointed when their new king, **James II**, who came to the throne after the death of Queen Elizabeth, announced he would pursue a policy of peace with Spain. The foundations of English naval power had been laid during the Elizabethan period, and it was only a matter of time before the English would contest with the Spanish, French and Dutch for mastery in the New World.

King Philip II

Religious differences simmered throughout the sixteenth century. In the seventeenth century they boiled over into a war that involved nearly all the major powers of Europe. The Holy Roman Empire, founded in 962 by **Otto the Great**, was fragmented between a largely **Protestant** northern section and a decidedly **Catholic** segment to the south. The war began when Czech patriots in Prague threw the commissioners of the Holy Roman Emperor out a window; the commissioners landed in a dung heap, and so the affair was known as the **Defenestration of Prague**.

At first, the war was strictly between Catholic Czechoslovakia and Protestant Bohemia. The Catholics won the early battles, virtually stamping out Protestantism in the eastern sections of the Holy Roman Empire. A new army entered the fray from the north: **Gustavus Adolphus**, the **Lutheran** King of **Sweden**, led a small, but well trained army south into the Holy Roman Empire. Giving

Cardinal Richelieu

support and assistance to the Protestant cause, Adolphus won two major victories over his foes before his death at the **Battle of Lutzen** in 1632.

France entered the war in 1635, not on the side of Catholicism, as might have been expected, but as an ally of the Protestants. **Cardinal Duc de Richelieu (1585-1642)**, the power behind the throne in France, wanted France to replace Spain as the foremost military power in Europe. Since Spain saw its role as upholding Catholic interests throughout Europe, France therefore lent its support the Protestant cause. Thereafter, the war began to disintegrate into power struggles in which religion played a smaller and smaller part. The Protestant Netherlands continued to fight for their independence from Catholic Spain (see no. 39); Protestant forces within the Holy Roman Empire continued to contest for mastery with **Ferdinand II**, the Catholic Hapsburg Emperor; Spain continued to send assistance to the Holy Roman Emperor, while France sent troops to assist the Protestants within the Empire.

By 1640 the contest was drawing to a close. Spain gathered its forces and attempted to drive France from the war. Instead, some of the very best Spanish troops were defeated or captured at the **Battle of Rocroi** in 1643. By 1648, all the sides involved were weary; the **Treaty of Westphalia** enacted in 1648, ended the struggle within the Empire with the clause that declared each prince could determine the religion his subjects would have to follow. Since the Empire had over 300 different princedoms, dukedoms, bishoprics, and principalities, there was room for the different faiths to be practiced. The Netherlands won their full and complete independence from Spain, and France and Spain continued to fight sporadically until 1659, when the **Treaty of the Pyrenees** ended their conflict.

Killing a king, known as regicide, was a fearsome thought to most Europeans. The English were the first Europeans to commit an act of regicide, during the long and bitter **Civil War** fought between the forces of King **Charles I (1600-1649)** and **Parliament**.

During the 1620s and 1630s, King Charles I came into serious conflict with Parliament. Charles demanded new taxes and levies that Parliament refused to grant, so the king dissolved Parliament and sought to run the kingdom by himself. Hamstrung by his inability to raise new taxes, Charles summoned a new Parliament in 1640. When he tried to dissolve that one--and to arrest five of its leading members--the English Civil War began between the **Cavaliers** (men loyal to the king) and **Roundheads** (those loyal to Parliament).

The war started with the **Battle of Edgehill** in 1642. The cavalry section of the king's army nearly won at the outset, but wasted time looting the wagon train of the enemy. The solid infantry of the Parliamentary forces then gained the field in a sharply contested fight. Edgehill was in many ways a precursor of the war as a whole. The Cavaliers generally fought with dash and verve, and often they were able to scatter their opponents' cavalry in the early stages of battles. The stronger discipline of the Roundheads, as well as their greater number of resources, enabled them to prevail in the

King Charles I

long run. The outcome of the war was very much in doubt until **Oliver Cromwell (1599-1658)** emerged as the primary leader of the Roundheads.

A severe man who believed wholeheartedly in the Puritan faith, Cromwell was so strict that he forbade his men to swear. He developed a cavalry force, the "Ironsides," as good as the horsemen of King Charles. The Roundheads won the **Battle of Marston Moor** in northern England in 1644, and **Prince Rupert of the Rhine**, swore vengeance. When the two forces met again at the **Battle of Naseby** in 1645, Rupert's cavalrymen repeated many of the same errors they had made at Edgehill and other conflicts. By the end of the day, the Parliamentary forces had won a complete victory, and the king was in flight.

King Charles surrendered to Parliament in 1645. Later, he was found to be in collusion with the Scots, who were planning a march south to liberate him. Cromwell hastened north and defeated the Scots soundly at the **Battle of Dunbar** in 1648. After returning to England, Cromwell pulled together a court of over 200 men to try the King. Since monarchy was so revered, many of these judges evaded the proceedings, but Cromwell's will prevailed in the end, with 59 judges signing the death warrant. King Charles was condemned for crimes against the state and executed on January 27, 1649.

King **Philip** of the **Narragansett** tribe in **Rhode Island** (he was known as **Metacomet** to his own people) was one of the first **Native American** chieftains to understand how insatiable the **English** colonists were for land. As a counter, he built a confederacy between his tribe and several others in the New England area, planning to deliver a blow against the English when the time was right.

The **Plymouth colony** settlers suspected Philip of plotting against them, and ordered him to present himself at Plymouth for trial. Philip refused, and a militia force was sent to capture him. That began what became known as **King Philip's War.** Lacking time to consolidate his confederacy, Philip fled from Rhode Island and began a series of devastating raids against English towns in central and western Massachusetts. **Brookfield** was one of

The Death of King Philip

the first towns attacked; followed by other towns such as **Leominster**.

By the fall of 1675, King Philip and his warriors had the English colonists on the run. Moving to western Massachusetts, King Philip undertook a major attack on **Hadley** in September. The "Angel of Hadley" has never been authenticated or disproved by historians, but the story is that as the Indians attacked, the townspeople were rallied by the appearance of an old man wielding a sword; by the time the Indians were chased off, the old man had disappeared. It is possible, though by no means certain, that the man in question was **William Goffe**, one of the 59 judges who had sentenced King **Charles I (1600-1649)** to death, and who had taken refuge in the New World when King **Charles II** ascended the throne in 1660 at the end of **Oliver Cromwell's (1599-1658)** rule (see no. 42).

King Philip's fortunes took a turn for the worse during the winter, when the fierce **Mohawk** warriors of the **Iroquois** tribes turned against him and attacked his people along the Mohawk Trail. In the spring of 1676, English soldiers from Hadley and Northampton attacked the main Indian settlement at what was known as the **Great Falls** (now Turners Falls, Massachusetts). Catching the Indians by surprise, the English killed as many as 300 people, many of them women and children.

As the heart went out of the Indians in western Massachusetts, King Philip returned to the Rhode Island border, where he was hunted down and killed by the colonists in August 1676. It was believed that King Philip's wife and infant son were sold into slavery in the Caribbean, but recent research indicates they escaped and made their way to the Canadian border where many of King Philip's descendants live today.

44. WAR OF THE LEAGUE OF AUGSBURG
1689-1697

Louis XIV (1638-1715), the Sun King of France, was the most powerful and feared monarch of his day. When he sent his armies into the Palatinate section of western Germany in 1688, England and the United Provinces of the Netherlands declared war against France.

The war began in earnest in 1689 and soon spread to the New World and the Caribbean Sea. For the first time, European power politics had enlarged to the point where people as far away as the colony of New York and the island of Jamaica were influenced by events in London, Paris, and Amsterdam.

The war began auspiciously for France. The well-trained armies of Louis XIV occupied a section of western Germany and pressed attacks against the Dutch Netherlands. In North America, Count Frontenac, the governor of Canada, sent French and Indian war parties to attack and destroy English settlements at Schenectady, New York, Salmon Falls, New Hampshire, and present-day Portland, Maine. In response to these attacks, Puritan New Englanders sailed up the Bay of Fundy and captured Port Royal, Acadia in the summer of 1690. Emboldened by this success, a second Puritan fleet left Boston and sailed to besiege Quebec City. Arriving at the city in early October, the Massachusetts forces soon had to withdraw because of the oncoming winter. Louis XIV had a medal struck to commemorate the successful defense of the city.

French naval forces reached their acme in 1690, when they defeated an English fleet in the Battle of Beachy Head, off the southern coast of England in 1690. The war soon settled into a series of stalemates: France won many victories on land;

England gained the edge at sea with a victory at Barfleur Bay in 1692; the fighting in the New World diminished to a series of raids and counter-raids. Count Frontenac was successful in inflicting a punishing attack against the Iroquois Indian tribes who were allied with the English in 1696, but the French and English virtually fought each other to a draw in the New World.

Peace negotiations began in 1696 and concluded in 1697 with the signing of the Peace of Ryswick. All territory that had been taken by either side during the war was returned to the other under the principle of Status Quo Ante Bellum (things returned to the way they had been). Louis XIV had been prevented from taking over Germany and Holland, but his ambitions on the continent of Europe had not ended.

King Louis XIV

GREAT NORTHERN WAR
1700-1721

As the eighteenth century dawned, Sweden was still the foremost military and commercial power on the Baltic Sea. Due to its intervention in the **Thirty Years' War** (see no. 41), Sweden controlled much of the shipping in the Baltic and had the most professional army in the region, despite its small population of one million.

When a fifteen-year-old boy became King **Charles XII (1682-1718)** of Sweden in 1697, the neighboring countries decided the time had come to put Sweden in its place. **Frederick IV** of Denmark, **Augustus II (1670-1733)** of Poland, and Czar **Peter I (1672-1725)** of Russia, later known as **Peter the Great**, formed a coalition against Sweden. The war began in 1700, when the Poles besieged the key city of **Riga** and the Russians did the same with **Narva**. The allies had underestimated the personality of the boy king of Sweden.

King Charles XII was a military genius as well as a megalomaniac. He attacked Denmark first, captured Copenhagen, and the Danes sought peace. He turned next to Russia, raised the siege of Narva and inflicted a humiliating defeat on the larger Russian army there. He moved on to relieve Riga and proceeded to seize **Warsaw** and **Cracow**, the major cities of Poland. After his decisive defeat of the Polish army at **Pultusk**, in April 1703, Charles persuaded the Polish legislature to elect his handpicked candidate as the new king in place of Augustus, who had fled to Saxony.

Charles left Sweden with 80,000 men in September 1707 and marched on Moscow. Deterred by the hard winter, he waited in the Ukraine. He was then defeated by Peter the Great at the crucial **Battle of Poltava** on June 28, 1709. Escaping with around 1,800 men, Charles went south to Turkey and managed to persuade the Ottoman Empire to start a war against Russia. The **Russo-Turkish War** lasted only two years, while back in northern Europe, Sweden faced a new coalition of its enemies: Poland, Russia, Saxony, Hanover and Denmark. Augustus II returned to his Polish throne and continued the war with a vengeance. Charles traveled incognito to Sweden in 1714; arriving in his homeland, he soon inspired his countrymen to further efforts. His brilliant, though erratic genius, might have turned the tide, but he was shot dead in the trenches while preparing to besiege the Norwegian fortress of **Fredrikssten** in December 1718.

The Swedish war effort soon ground to a halt. The **Treaties of Stockholm** from 1719 to 1720 and of **Nystad** in 1721, yielded Livonia, Ingermanland, part of Karelia, and many Baltic islands to Russia, which in turn gave up Finland. Czar Peter the Great emerged as the clear winner. At a huge cost in lives and treasure, Russia had gained a Baltic port, the "window to the west" that Peter wanted, and he soon built the city of **St. Petersburg** to commemorate his achievement. Russia became the dominant power in the Baltic Sea, and Sweden never regained the military position it had held in the second half of the seventeenth century.

Charles XII at Poltava

After King **Charles II (1661-1700)** of Spain died without a legal heir, both France and Austria claimed title to the Spanish throne. If the throne went to France, it would make the already large possessions of King **Louis XIV (1638-1715)** absolutely immense; if it went to Austria, France would be bracketed by two hostile countries, one to the south and one to the east. Louis XIV decided to risk all and stake his claim to the Spanish throne. Giving just enough leeway for his foes to feel secure, he gave up his own claim and asserted that of his grandson, **Philip of Anjou,** who soon became King of Spain and all the Spanish possessions in the New World.

William III

Led by King **William III (1650-1702)** of England, a coalition of countries arose to challenge the might of France and Spain. England, the Netherlands, and Austria were the most prominent members of the **Grand Alliance,** designed to thwart Louis XIV's plans for continental mastery. Upon King William's death, the coalition was headed by Queen **Anne (1665-1714)** of England; hence, the conflict is called **Queen Anne's War** in North America.

From the start, the coalition had the advantage in numbers and leadership. The French generals were old and their strategies out of date compared with the battle plans of the two great Allied commanders: **John Churchill (1650-1722)** of England (later the first **Duke of Marlborough**) and **Prince Eugene of Savoy.** Churchill won an over-whelming victory at **Blenheim** in 1704; it was followed by other triumphs at **Ramillies** in 1706, **Oudenarde** in 1708, and **Malpaquet** in 1709. Even more seriously, the allies captured **Gibraltar** in 1704 and actually invaded and held large sections of Spain during the war. The aged King Louis XIV was so discouraged that he sued for peace in 1709, but upon learning that the allies insisted he take up arms against his grandson in Spain, Louis XIV decided to fight on. His armies won an important victory at **Denain** in 1711, which allowed France to exit the war with some dignity.

In **North America**, the English and French employed Indian allies (Abenaki with the French, Iroquois with the English) to harass one another's towns and settlements; both sides were happy to learn that the **Peace of Utrecht** had been signed in 1713. France yielded Nova Scotia and Newfoundland to Great Britain; Spain surrendered Gibraltar and the right to transport African slaves to the Spanish colonies in South America to Britain, and the territories on the Continent reverted to the country that had controlled them before the war began. The war made Britain into the world's number one sea power, and seriously weakened France's bid for hegemony on the Continent. Louis XIV died two years after the war ended, having outlived his son and grandson; his five-year-old great-grandson succeeded him as Louis XV.

47. WAR OF JENKINS' EAR
1739-1744

In 1739, **Robert Jenkins**, a British merchant captain, appeared before the British Parliament and told a story of how he had been humiliated and mutilated by a Spanish revenue officer off the coast of Spanish South America. British captains had routinely overstepped their trading rights in South America since the **War of the Spanish Succession** (see no. 46), and Jenkins was one of the few who paid a penalty; losing his ear to the scrod of the revenue officer. Parliament reacted with an uproar, and Prime Minister **Robert Walpole (1697-1762)** was forced to lead the country into a war against Spain. The peace-loving Walpole's comment was, "They're ringing the bells now, they'll be wringing their hands soon."

Robert Walpole

Spain had rebuilt its naval forces under the new Bourbon monarchy that began with Philip V in 1702. Knowing that Britain would attack its colonies in the **Caribbean** and **South America**, Spain sent armies and fleets to defend those areas. The war was largely confined to the colonies and open seas; there was almost no fighting in Europe. Spain defended its colonies with considerable skill, while Britain continued to show the great predominance it had on the oceans of the world. British Captain **George Anson (1697-1762)** sailed to the bottom of South America, rounded the Horn, and preyed on Spanish shipping on the west coast of South America. He then sailed across the Pacific Ocean (capturing the famed Spanish Manila galleon along the way), and returned to England by circumnavigating the globe; he was the third naval captain to achieve this feat (Magellan and Sir Francis Drake were the first two).

Britain's 13 colonies in **North America** contributed to the war effort. In 1743, a large British fleet picked up 3,000 to 4,000 American militiamen from the colonies and sailed to besiege the Spanish fortress city of **Cartagena**, on the northern coast of South America. The siege was a debacle; the city was not taken, and nearly three-quarters of the colonists died from disease during the fruitless campaign. The whole affair did much to create negative feelings between British and American soldiers.

The war did not end, but instead blended in with the **War of the Austrian Succession** (see no. 48) in 1744. Neither Britain nor Spain could claim victory as a result.

Charles of Lorraine, king of Austria, died in 1740, leaving the throne to his daughter, **Maria Theresa (1717-1780)**. Prior to his death, the king had gained written promises from other European powers that they would respect his daughter's right to the throne. The promises, called the **Pragmatic Sanction**, were rejected by the new King of Prussia, **Frederick II (1712-1786)**, soon to be known as **Frederick the Great**. Disdaining a woman on the throne, Frederick moved rapidly to take **Silesia**, a coal-rich province of Austria, away from her. Since Maria Theresa was at the same time facing a potential rebellion by her Hungarian subjects (descendants of the Magyars who had invaded Europe in the ninth century), she was powerless to stop Frederick; instead she sought allies and planned her revenge.

Great Britain made alliance with Austria, while France joined briefly with Prussia. This meant a full-scale war on the European continent, one that spread to the world's oceans and the colonies of France, England and Spain. Britain and Spain had already fought for four years in the **War of Jenkins' Ear** (see no. 47).

Frederick the Great consolidated his conquest of Silesia, while French armies besieged a number of Dutch cities and came close to overrunning the whole of the Netherlands. It was at sea and in the New World that the consequences of the war (called **King George's War** in North America) were the most profound. British-American farmers and fishermen captured the French fortress of **Louisbourg** on Cape Breton Island in 1745 and British fleets won significant victories over the French in 1747.

The war ended in a draw between England and France. In the peace **Treaty of Aix-la-Chapelle**, signed in 1748, France and Britain returned to each other all the territory they had conquered; Louisbourg was exchanged for Madras in India. The French yielded the expansive conquests they had made in the Netherlands. The only leader who seemed to gain anything from the war was Frederick II of Prussia, who maintained his hold on Silesia, with its one million subjects and rich deposits of coal and iron ore. Maria Theresa swore revenge on Frederick, and the diplomatic maneuvering that followed soon led to another conflict; the **Seven Years' War** (see no. 49).

Capture of the Austrians by Frederick's Dragoons

49. THE SEVEN YEARS' WAR
1756-1763

William Pitt

In 1754, events in North America started a brushfire that escalated into the bonfire of the **Seven Years' War** in Europe, India and on the oceans of the globe.

At age 21, **George Washington (1732-1799)** ambushed a small detachment of French soldiers in western Pennsylvania in May 1754. Both Britain and France sent large bodies of soldiers across the Atlantic Ocean to contest for control of the "Ohio country"-- present-day western Pennsylvania, Ohio, and Indiana. French and Indian fighters ambushed the British-Americans in what became known as **Braddock's defeat** in Pennsylvania in 1755, and a full-scale war followed, known in America as the **French and Indian War**.

In Europe, traditional alliances were cast aside. Longtime enemies France and Austria joined together, while Britain and Prussia became partners. This switch of allies from the previous war, known as the **Diplomatic Revolution** of 1756, almost guaranteed a long and destructive conflict. Russia joined on the side of France and Austria a short time later.

Frederick II (1712-1786), also known as **Frederick the Great** won battle after battle on the Continent. His great tactical skill, combined with the professionalism and determination of his forces, enabled Prussia to fight off attacks by her far more numerous enemies.

Great Britain sought to use her naval power to contain France in Europe and capture French colonies elsewhere around the globe. The British failed at first, and French armies won notable victories in North America at **Oswego** in 1756 and **Fort William Henry** in 1757.

The tide turned when **William Pitt (1708-1778)** became Prime Minister of Great Britain in 1757. Convinced that "I know I can save this country, and no one else can," Pitt redoubled the British efforts. Giving money to Frederick II so that the Prussians could contain the French power in Europe, Pitt sent out armies and fleets that won victory after victory at **Quebec**, **Minden**, **Ticonderoga**, and **Quiberon Bay**. Known as the **Year of Victories**, 1759 set the stage for the creation of the British empire.

The entrance of Bourbon Spain into the war in 1761 did not make much difference. British fleets and armies soon captured Havana, Cuba and the Philippines, making Spain rue the day she had sought to assist her fellow Bourbon monarchy in France. The **Peace of Paris** that ended the war in 1763 gave all of Canada and India to Great Britain; France was left with only two small islands off the coast of Newfoundland for fishing purposes. Frederick II retained Silesia; while France, Austria and Russia had almost nothing to show for seven long years of warfare.

The powerful Russian empire developed by **Peter the Great (1672-1725)** came close to destruction in the late eighteenth century from an internal rebellion. **Pugachev's Revolt**, begun in 1773, nearly toppled Czarina **Catherine the Great (1729-1796)**; its failure led to a society characterized by a greater class disparity than before.

Yemelyan Ivanovich Pugachev (poo-ga-chof) was a Don Cossack who served in the Russo-Turkish war of 1768 to 1774. Wounded in the war, he began to wander through southern Russia, preaching "Old Believer" doctrine, that is, the beliefs of the Orthodox Russia that had existed prior to the reign of Peter the Great. Finding that discontented serfs, escaped convicts, and even Cossacks were willing to listen to him, Pugachev promised freedom and land to those who would follow him. Briefly imprisoned for desertion from the Russian army, he escaped in May 1773, and by September of that year he had assembled the nucleus of a guerrilla force. In the months that followed, he was joined by thousands of Russians who were eager to do something to change Russian society; serfdom had greatly increased in the first 10 years of Czarina Catherine's reign.

Claiming to be Czar **Peter III** (Catherine's deranged husband, whom she had murdered in 1762), Pugachev increased the size of his following. In 1774, he besieged, but did not capture, Orenburg; in the Volga region, he managed to sack both **Kazan** and **Sotov**. The Russian elite in Moscow felt threatened, and Catherine sent her best troops and most effective generals to combat the rebels. Count **Alexander Suvurov** defeated Pugachev's forces at the **Battle of Tzaritsyn** in September 1774, ending the chance for the revolt to succeed.

Pugachev escaped from the battlefield and made his way to the Ural Mountains, where he was betrayed and handed over to the royal forces. He was brought in an iron cage to Moscow where he was executed on January 11, 1775, just three months prior to the start of the **American Revolution**. The rebellion achieved the opposite of its intention: Catherine became increasingly distrustful of her people, and serfdom increased during the remainder of her years in power. Catherine, who had originally been attracted to the ideas of the **Enlightenment**--even inviting the philosopher **Diderot** to live with her in St. Petersburg--became instead a firm believer in autocracy as the only means of controlling the people. The rebellion increased Russia's movement toward absolute monarchy, bolstered by a boyar class that subsisted on the backs of the serfs, who would not be freed until 1861.

Catherine the Great

George Washington

The **Revolutionary War** began in April 1775, when Patriot militiamen returned the fire of British redcoats at **Lexington Green** and **Concord Bridge**. Starting as a New England affair, with the fighting centered in and around Boston, the war broadened when the Continental Congress named 42-year-old **George Washington (1732-1799)** commander-in-chief of the American forces. Being a Virginian, Washington brought a sense of intercolonial unity to the American rebellion, unity furthered by the broadsides of **Thomas Paine (1737-1809)** and the elegant phrasing of **Thomas Jefferson's (1743-1826) Declaration of Independence**. By late 1776, the rebellion had turned into a true revolution.

Americans were almost on their last legs. Washington's defeats at Long Island, New York City, and his subsequent retreat to New Jersey made the American cause seem truly desperate toward the end of the year. It was Washington's bold Christmas gamble of crossing the Delaware, which led to the American victory at **Trenton**, that restored some measure of hope to the Americans.

In the spring and summer of 1777, British armies sought to converge on Albany and cut the rebel states (no longer colonies) in half. Heroic leadership by men such as **Benedict Arnold (1741-1801)** and **Daniel Morgan** as well as several errors by the British led to the surrender of over 7,000 British and Hessian soldiers at **Saratoga** in October 1777. That American victory brought France in as an American ally, changing the war into a worldwide conflict, with battles fought from India to the Caribbean.

Early attempts at Franco-American cooperation led to disastrous defeats at Savannah, Georgia and Newport, Rhode Island. Sensing that the Americans were losing heart, the British shifted tactics and attacked in the Southern states, while holding the line in and around New York City in the north. The British enjoyed notable successes until they were challenged by the last and best hope of the Americans in the south: General **Nathanael Greene**. A brilliant strategist, Greene led the British on hide-and-seek marches throughout the Carolinas. Believing his men could be resupplied by ship, British General **Charles Cornwallis (1738-1805)** led his army to the small tobacco town of **Yorktown** on Chesapeake Bay.

The French had briefly gained control of the waters of Chesapeake Bay. While the French fleet prevented Cornwallis' escape by sea, American and French troops marched south from the New York City area and placed the British army in the vise grips of a classic, European-style siege. On October 19, 1781, Cornwallis surrendered his entire army. The **Treaty of Paris** of 1783 ended the war by recognizing American independence.

"I am not numbered among that common herd of statesmen...who have yet to learn that there is no compounding with tyrants, who have yet to learn that the only place to strike a king is between head and shoulders, who have yet to learn that they will get nothing from Europe except by force of arms. I vote for the tyrant's death." So said **George Danton**, philosopher and spokesperson for the French revolutionaries who executed King **Louis XVI** in January 1793. Following three years of revolutionary activity, the Legislative Assembly tried the king, found him guilty of crimes against the state, and sent him to the gallows. It was only the second time in European history that a people had sent their monarch to his death: the first had occurred when **Charles I (1600-1649)** of England was executed by **Oliver Cromwell's (1599-1658)** Roundhead followers (see no. 42).

Within a few months of the death of Louis XVI, France found itself at war with Great Britain, Spain, Prussia and Austria. The odds of the revolution surviving such a storm were small, especially since the officers corps of France's pre-Revolutionary army had been made up entirely of members of the nobility, who were now excluded from the new citizen army.

Lucien Carnot came forward to provide the leadership France needed. Determined to save the revolution from extinction by the monarchies of Europe, he declared a national emergency and created what was called the **Levee en Masse**, in which all able-bodied males were required to serve the nation. Young men fought on the battlefield, middle-aged men forged weapons in factories, and old men were required to ring bells in town squares and shout patriotic slogans such as "Vive le Republic!"

In 1793, Carnot managed to mobilize 800,000 Frenchmen and organize them into

Louis XVI on the scaffold

an army. It was a force of unheard-of size; even the armies of Louis XIV a century earlier had never exceeded 400,000. With revolutionary enthusiasm and new battle tactics (such as imitating the fighting style of the North American Indians), the French began to defeat their more "professional" foes in battle after battle. By early 1794, France had pushed the invaders out of the eastern areas of the country. In the same year a young colonel named **Napoleon Bonaparte (1769-1821)** showed his deftness in the use of artillery when he forced the British fleet to end its occupation of the French Mediterranean port of Toulon.

The **Committee of Safety**, which had organized the Levee en Masse, was replaced by the **Directory** government in 1795. The new rulers of France sent even larger armies forth that not only drove the enemies away, but also began to acquire large sections of land in Switzerland, Italy, the Holy Roman Empire and the Netherlands. By 1798, the armies of the French Republic had achieved all that Louis XIV had wanted: the "natural boundaries of France."

Grand Army leaving the Kremlin

Napoleon Bonaparte (1769-1821) became First Consul of France in 1800, following a series of remarkable victories in northern Italy, as well as a disastrous campaign in Egypt that cost him an entire army. After 10 years of revolution, warfare and sacrifice, the French people wanted stability, and Napoleon seemed the man to provide it.

Born in Corsica to a family of the lower nobility, Napoleon was insatiably ambitious. He continued France's ongoing war with England until 1803, when he obtained peace with honor in the **Treaty of Amiens**. When Britain refused to agree to his takeover of **Malta**, Napoleon went to war again, intent on crushing Great Britain.

The British fleet wiped out the French fleet at the **Battle of Trafalgar** in 1805, effectively ending any chance for the French to invade England. Napoleon turned his attention to the Continent and fought a series of battles that completely defeated the Prussians and Austrians in 1806. He then fought against Czarist Russia; although the battles were

inconclusive, Napoleon wound up befriending Czar **Alexander I (1777-1825)** and persuaded him to join in a boycott of British trade goods.

In 1808, Napoleon allowed himself to become engaged in a futile war to place his younger brother **Joseph** on the throne of Spain. Britain, seeing an opening in the Napoleonic control of Europe, landed troops in Portugal. Under the leadership of **Arthur Wellesley (1769-1852)**, later known as the **Duke of Wellington**, the British foiled every attempt made by different French marshals to drive them from the Iberian peninsula. By 1810, the French control of the Continent was beginning to falter.

Sensing a loss of momentum, Napoleon gathered an army of 600,000 men, and marched on Russia, determined to overthrow Czar Alexander, who had failed to completely boycott British goods. Napoleon and his army were instead overwhelmed by the size of the Russian landscape, the determination of the Russian armies, and the ferocity of the winter of 1812 to 1813. Only 50,000 men who had marched against Russia returned.

Surrounded by his many foes, Napoleon fought brilliantly during 1813, but in 1814 he yielded to the inevitable and abdicated his throne as emperor. He was given the island of **Elba** in the Mediterranean to rule.

Napoleon escaped from Elba in 1815 and returned to France, where the population welcomed him once again as their emperor. Fighting against a coalition of British, Prussian and Austrian forces, he lost the day at the **Battle of Waterloo**, June 18, 1815. This time the British sent him to the tiny island of **St. Helena** in the southern Atlantic Ocean. He spent the rest of his life writing a memoir. When he died, an era ended in which one man had risen to greatness and presided over the continent of Europe.

"From the halls of Montezuma to the shores of **Tripoli**," is from the official song of the **United States Marine Corps**, but few Americans know what brought Americans to the shores of Tripoli in the first years of the nineteenth century.

The Barbary pirates, based in the North African cities of Algiers, Tunis and Tripoli, had made their living by piracy for centuries. Many countries--including the young United States--found it more convenient to pay a few million dollars in tribute, rather than fight against the pirates. The **Pasha of Tripoli** determined that the Americans were especially weak, and in 1801, he had his men cut down the flagpole of the American embassy in his city, which was his method of declaring war.

American President **Thomas Jefferson (1743-1826)** was a pacifist at heart, but he was also a pragmatist. Rather than conciliating the Barbary states or pay any more tribute, he ordered frigates and sloops of the newly launched **United States Navy** to sail to the Mediterranean and fight against Tripoli.

The first American squadron blockaded the port and engaged in inconclusive fighting. The second squadron, the frigate **USS Philadelphia**, ran aground on a reef, was captured by the Barbary pirates and brought to Tripoli as a prize. The Tripolitans intended to use the frigate as a model to construct frigates of their own, which would have rendered the American fleet almost useless. American lieutenant **Stephen Decatur (1779-1820)** led a small number of men into the harbor of Tripoli at night and burned the Philadelphia to the waterline.

Decatur also led a series of attacks on Tripolitan gunboats in the harbor, but it was left to an ambitious New Englander, **William Eaton**, and eight United States Marines to strike the final blow against Tripoli. Landing in Alexandria, Egypt, Eaton recruited allies and marched across the Libyan desert to the port city of **Derna**. After capturing the city, Eaton found that the Pasha of Tripoli was willing to negotiate with the Americans. A treaty was signed in 1805, ending the former tribute payments and the war itself.

The Barbary pirates carried out raids again, while the United States was occupied with the **War of 1812** (see no. 55), but a visit by Commodore Decatur and a number of American frigates in 1815 ended that threat. The **Tripolitan War** and its aftermath started off a winning tradition for the United States Navy and Marine Corps.

Stephen Decatur

55. WAR OF 1812
1812-1814

Sometimes called the "War of Faulty Communication," the **War of 1812** took place in an international atmosphere of distrust and confusion.

The United States declared war on Great Britain on June 18, 1812, in response to the British practice of boarding American merchant ships and pressing American seamen into service against their will. Unknown to President **James Madison (1751-1836)** and Congress, British Prime Minister **Spencer Perceval (1762-1812)** had been assassinated in May, and the new British cabinet was willing to retract the infamous **Orders-in-Council** that had led to impressment in the first place. A British ship arrived in New York City with the news, unfortunately a few days too late to influence events.

Americans hoped to seize British Canada. With a population of only 500,000, the Canadians would have had a hard time resisting a cohesive American attack. Cohesion, however, was the problem: the American

Perry's victory on Lake Erie

commanders were past their prime--and the American militia refused to cross the border into Canada, claiming that their enlistment contracts did not require them to serve beyond the limits of their states. Early American offensives went nowhere, and the British actually captured **Fort Detroit** and a substantial American garrison.

The Americans had better luck at sea, where the well-built frigates of the fledgling Navy did well in ship-to-ship battles against the British.

During 1813, the status quo held in the New York/Ontario area, but the Americans won an important naval battle on **Lake Erie**, and Shawnee Chief **Tecumseh** (an important ally of the British) was killed in the **Battle of the Thames River**. The Americans were gaining the upper hand throughout 1813, but in the spring of 1814, they learned that **Napoleon Bonaparte (1769-1821)** had abdicated his throne. Thousands of battle-hardened British veterans were being shipped to America.

British troops occupied and burnt part of **Washington, DC** in August 1814, but were repulsed at **Baltimore** in September, an event that gave birth to the song that would later become the national anthem. British forces crossed into New York state as well, but retreated when the Americans defeated the British fleet on **Lake Champlain**. That left one more possible opening for the British: an attack on the important merchant city of New Orleans.

British troops advanced to within five miles of the city in December 1814, not knowing that the peace **Treaty of Ghent** had been signed on December 24. The **Battle of New Orleans** on January 8, 1815, was a debacle for the British who lost 2,000 men killed, wounded or missing in an attack on American defenders led by **Andrew Jackson**.

The revolution that freed **Peru** from Spanish rule was actually instigated by outside forces. Peru had been a bastion of Spanish authority in the New World since **Francisco Pizarro's (1470-1541)** conquest in 1532. Home to the Spanish treasure fleets and remote from the outside world, Peru remained under the Spanish thumb longer than some of its South American neighbors.

Jose de San Martin (1778-1850), an Argentine who had liberated Chile from Spanish rule, brought 5,000 Argentine and Chilean troops by ship to landfall at Pisco, Peru in 1820. San Martin's troops camped at Huacho, where they were joined by many Peruvian recruits; the arrival of the soldiers had galvanized support for revolution. The Spanish viceroy fled from the capital city of Lima to the Sierra mountains, and there gathered his forces. The citizens of Lima opened the gates to San Martin in July, and on July 28, 1821, he proclaimed the independence of Peru. Knowing he needed allies, San Martin appealed to the Colombian patriot and revolutionary **Simon Bolivar (1783-1830)**. Bolivar and San Martin met at Guayaquil from July 26 to 27, and San Martin turned over control of the movement to Bolivar. In 1822, San Martin returned to Argentina, leaving his army in Peru.

In the absence of San Martin, the viceroy of Peru bolstered his forces and prepared to retake Lima. Bolivar and his lieutenant,

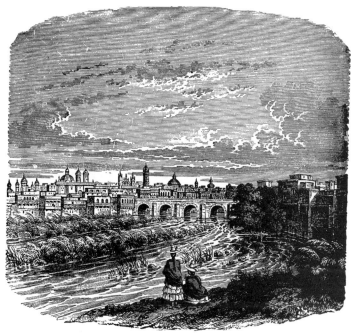

Lima, Peru

Antonio Jose de Sucre, arrived in Peru in 1823 with a small army of Colombians and Venezuelans. On August 6, 1824, Bolivar and Sucre defeated a royalist army at the **Battle of Junin**. Completing the revolutionary success, Sucre led 6,000 men in the **Battle of Ayacucho** on December 9, 1824, where nearly the entire Spanish army of 9,000 men was captured. Spanish envoys soon agreed to remove all troops from Peru. In Upper Peru, revolutionaries defeated the remaining 4,000 royalist troops, ending the war. Sucre had made a prior agreement with the leaders of **Upper Peru** to create two separate countries; in order to pacify Bolivar, who wanted one country, Sucre named Upper Peru, **Bolivia**. Sucre became the first president of Bolivia, one of the only two landlocked South American countries.

Having felt the tramp of the Spanish boot since the time of **Hernando Cortez (1485-1547)** (see no. 37), the people of Mexico--Peninsulare, Creole, Mestizo and Indian--yearned for freedom. The opportunity to win that freedom was provided by the havoc the **Napoleonic Wars** (see no. 53) caused in Europe, and in Spain in particular.

King **Ferdinand VII** of Spain was restored to his throne following the impeachment of **Napoleon Bonaparte (1769-1821)** but the

King Ferdinand VII

Spanish monarchy had been greatly weakened by its exile from Madrid. Seeing the lack of central authority in Spain, Mexicans began to seek their independence, and rebel forces formed. **Augustin de Iturbide** was given command of 2,500 Spanish soldiers to find and defeat guerrillas led by **Vicente Guerrero**. The two men clashed in minor battles, but then joined forces and issued the **Plan of Iguala**, calling for an independent Mexican monarchy and racial equality for all Mexicans. The latter clause attracted the attention of thousands of Mexicans and other rebel leaders. Most of the regular Spanish army began to desert under the pressure, and Viceroy **Juan O'Donoju** signed the **Treaty of Cordoba** with Iturbide in 1821, ending Spanish rule and establishing Mexican independence. After finding himself proclaimed Mexican emperor by his own soldiers, Iturbide crowned himself on May 19, 1822, creating the first **Empire of Mexico**.

The new empire did not last. Iturbide found it difficult to collect revenues and duties, since a small Spanish garrison still controlled the fortress of **San Juan de Ulloa** off Vercaruz. Sending a force of soldiers under the command of General **Antonio Lopez de Santa Anna (1795-1876)** to capture the fortress, Iturbide soon learned that Santa Anna had claimed command of the entire army and declared a Mexican republic. In February 1823, Santa Anna and General **Guadalupe Victoria** issued the **Plan de Casa Mata**, calling for a new constitution and government. The Mexican army seemed inclined to favor the plan, and Iturbide abdicated his throne in March 1823. The first Mexican republic was soon formed, with Guadalupe Victoria as the first president.

"The mountains look on Marathon,
And Marathon looks on the sea;
And musing there an hour alone,
I dreamed that Greece might still be free."

These words of author **Lord Byron**, written in 1818, illustrate the yearning of many European intellectuals to free Greece from the **Ottoman Empire**, which had held Athens, Marathon and the entire country of Greece since 1456. It was not an idle wish, since there were two resistance movements building within Greece itself. Nationalistic societies such as **Philike Hetairia** (Society of Friends), appealed to Greek intellectuals, while the **Klephts** mountaineers planned for a guerrilla-style war against the Turks.

The Greek revolution began in 1821, and achieved early successes that convinced Greek patriots to declare the independence of their country at **Epidaurus** on January 13, 1822. The Turks tried, but failed to capture the fortress of **Missolonghi** at the entrance to the Gulf of Corinth, and withdrew. Jubilant Greeks took and held **Tripolis** and **Athens** in 1822. The Greeks then paused to set up a civil government; during the interlude, the Ottoman sultan asked the **Pasha of Egypt** for assistance. The Pasha sent his son **Ibrahim** with Egyptian troops, and they captured Missolonghi in 1826, Athens in 1827, and recaptured the Morea. It appeared that the efforts of the Greeks could not prevail against the combined weight of the Ottoman Empire and Egypt.

The spirit of Romanticism and revolution, which had permeated Europe since the start

of the **French Revolution** (see no. 52), induced the leaders of Britain, France and Russia to sign a joint protocol, calling for Egypt to withdraw its troops. When both

Lord Byron

Constantinople and Egypt refused, the combined fleets of the three nations sailed into the Mediterranean and defeated the Turkish fleet at the **Battle of Navarino** on October 20, 1827. To further weaken the sultan's resolve, a Russo-Turkish war broke out in 1828. Eventually the Turks bowed to the inevitable. The **Treaty of Adrianople** in 1829 recognized the autonomy of Greece, and the **Treaty of London** in 1832 assured the independence of the country that had been under Ottoman rule for 376 years.

FRENCH CONQUEST OF ALGERIA
1830-1847

In 1830, many Frenchmen were bored with the uninspired rule of King **Charles X (1757-1836)**, and some even yearned for the days of **Napoleon Bonaparte (1769-1821)**, when France had been respected and feared for its military prowess. Aware of this malaise, Charles sent 37,000 soldiers to North Africa in June; the troops captured the city of **Algiers** on July 5.

This military adventure did not save Charles his reputation or his throne; he was overthrown in the same month by the citizens of Paris, who then proclaimed his cousin, **Louis Philippe (1773-1850)** of the House of Orleans, "King of the French."

The new king continued the Algerian venture, and on March 9, 1831, he signed an order creating **la Legion Etrangere**, ever since known to the world as the **French Foreign Legion**.

Four times the size of France, Algeria had a long history of tribal conflict. A remarkable leader emerged to challenge the French invasion. **Abd al-Qadir (1807?-1883)**, a Muslim leader and the emir of Mascara, led Algerians

of many different tribes in a war of harassment from 1832 to 1834 against French troops in **Oran** and **Mostaganem**. In 1834, the French signed the **Desmichels Treaty**, which recognized al-Qadir's position as emir and gave him control of the interior areas of Oran.

Continued French expansion from the coast led to a second war from 1835 to 1837 during which the French regular army and Foreign Legion fought many battles against al-Qadir's tribespeople. **The Treaty of Tafna** ended this second war and gave control of most of the interior to al-Qadir; the French retained only a few ports on the North African coast.

In December 1840, Marshal **Thomas R. Bugeaud** arrived as the new French commander in Algeria. Using new battle tactics such as the deployment of "flying columns" of lightly equipped troops, he drove al-Qadir's men into **Morocco**. The ever-resilient emir soon enlisted the Moroccans as allies and used cavalrymen to conduct incessant raids against the French. The showdown between Bugeaud and al-Qadir came at the **Battle of Isly** in east Morocco on August 14, 1844. Six thousand French infantry and 1,500 cavalrymen faced 45,000 Algerians in heat that climbed to 140 degrees Fahrenheit. The French won a decisive victory, and al-Qadir withdrew to Morocco with only a handful of men. A number of hard-fought skirmishes followed the battle of Isly, and in 1847, al-Qadir surrendered himself and his last followers to French General **Christophe Lamoriciere**.

A number of important skirmishes were fought after the surrender of al-Qadir but the heart had gone out of the resistance.

Battle of Isly

United States citizens began to cross the **Sabine River** into present-day Texas after 1820. Still fighting for its independence from Spain, Mexico welcomed the Norte Americanos and invited them to settle in Texas under two conditions: that they become Mexican citizens and convert to Catholicism. The Americans generally agreed to these terms, but were lax about satisfying either requirement.

In April 1830, Mexico banned the importation of any more slaves into Texas, imperiling the way of life that American settlers had brought to Texas: cotton production and plantations. The Americans refused to abide by this demand, and relations soon became strained between Texas and Mexico City. **Stephen Austin**, one of the first and most prominent Americans to settle in Texas, went to Mexico City, but was unable to work out a satisfactory agreement. When Mexican President **Antonio Lopez de Santa Anna (1795-1876)** annulled the 1824 constitution that had given significant autonomy to the individual Mexican states, the Americans declared that Texas was a nation independent from Mexico.

Santa Anna marched north with 6,000 Mexican soldiers, determined to quell the rebellion. He stopped to attack the old fortress called the **Alamo**, held by 184 Texans led by Colonel **William Travis**. When the Texans refused to surrender, a bloody siege ensued, from February 24 to March 6, 1836. The Mexicans finally stormed the fort and killed all of the defenders, but estimates of the Mexican losses run as high as 1,500 men killed, wounded or missing.

Santa Anna then proceeded southeast and captured 400 Americans at **Goliad**. The Americans surrendered under terms that promised normal treatment as prisoners of

Sam Houston

war. Instead, Santa Anna ordered their execution and had them blindfolded, bound and shot. The massacre at Goliad, much less well known than the siege of the Alamo, made the rebellion a matter of life or death for Texans.

Texan Colonel **Sam Houston (1793-1863)** collected a force of 1,500 Texans, who came to battle with the Mexicans at **San Jacinto** on April 21, 1836. Houston and his men attacked during the afternoon siesta, catching the Mexicans completely by surprise. The Mexicans were routed, and Santa Anna was captured.

The victory at San Jacinto gave independence to Texas. Santa Anna signed a treaty that granted freedom to the state and gained his own release. The Mexican government later disavowed the treaty. It was clear that the Texas question would have to wait for a resolution.

The three-year war between Great Britain and China began over opium, trade rights, and the traditional closed society of Imperial China. Both medicinal and a narcotic, opium was being produced in great quantities in **Indonesia** and **India**. British traders in India made fortunes by transporting the drug to China for sale; in fact, the number of chests of opium smuggled illegally into China increased from 4,244 in 1821 to 40,200 in 1839.

Opium Den

The **Manchu** dynasty, which ruled in China from 1644 to 1911, outlawed the importation of opium, and sent Imperial Commissioner **Lin Tse-hsu** to **Canton** to enforce the decree. On March 30, 1839, Tse-hsu forced foreign merchants residing in Canton to open their warehouses, and his agents proceeded to dump 20,000 chests full of opium valued at $6 million into the river. Since Canton was the only Chinese port that foreigners were allowed to trade with, it seemed quite possible that the Chinese could end the importation of opium into their country.

Always sensitive to the interests of its merchants, the British government sent a naval force to the Chinese coast; the opium trade from India to China was too valuable to be allowed to lapse. The British ships declared a blockade of all Chinese ports, and in May 1841, a British force moved up the Pearl River and captured Canton itself. The Chinese cities of **Amoy** and **Ningpo** fell soon afterward, but the British attacks soon wound down due to a lack of supplies, disease and typhoon-like weather.

In the spring of 1842, two new, energetic British commanders led in the capture of **Shanghai** and **Chinkiang**. By mid-1842, British marines under General **Hugh Gough**, and naval units led by Admiral **William Parker**, had seized the point where the Grand Canal intersected the Yangtze River and were in a position to threaten the grain supply of Peking itself. The Manchu leaders had no choice but to negotiate, and on August 29, 1842, China agreed to the **Treaty of Nanking**. Under its terms five Chinese ports--Canton, Amoy, Foochow, Ningpo and Shanghai--were to be opened to British merchants. The port of **Hong Kong** was ceded by China to Britain, diplomatic relations were to be conducted in the future on the basis of equality, and China was required to pay a $20 million fine for the destruction of the opium in the harbor and the costs of the war. The Treaty of Nanking was followed by treaties in 1844 that granted similar trading rights to French and American merchants. The Manchu dynasty suffered a serious loss of prestige, and China's view of itself as the Middle Kingdom, the center of all creation, was undermined by evidence that European warfare was more effective than that of the Chinese.

At the same time that Great Britain was involved in the **First Opium War** (see no. 61), she was also playing the "Great Game" with Czarist Russia; a competition to dominate India and Central Asia. Afghanistan, lodged directly between Russian and British forces, felt justly threatened from both powers and sought to maintain its independence, although it should be noted that Afghanistan was composed of tribal factions and not a true nation-state in the European sense.

The **Sadozai** family had ruled Afghanistan from 1747 to 1826; in the latter year, **Dost Mohammed** of the **Barotzai** clan took the throne as emir of Afghanistan. When the **Sikhs** of India began to press against the Afghan border in an attempt to conquer more territory, Dost Mohammed asked the British to intervene. Receiving no help from the British, he turned to the Russians with the same request. Upon hearing this, British leaders in India sent an army northward in 1839. The British captured **Kandahar** and **Ghazni**, and Dost Mohammed fled from the Afghan capital of **Kabul**. The British entered Kabul and placed **Shah Sooja** of the Sadozai family on the throne as the new emir. They failed to realize that to the Afghans, the emir was only a chief among chieftains, far from an absolute lord. Harassed by guerrilla warfare, the British withdrew from Kabul on January 6, 1842, with a force of 4,500 British and Bengali troops, accompanied by 12,500 camp followers.

Almost immediately after leaving Kabul on their march to **Jalalabad**, the British and their allies were set upon by thousands of Afghan tribesmen, who used the advantage of the rough terrain to overpower the British. The

Afghan Warrior

retreat turned into a complete rout, and by January 13, the entire army and its array of camp followers had been slain. The sole known survivor was a British surgeon, **William Brydon**, whose exhausted pony brought him to Jalalabad, where he delivered the news that the garrison had been wiped out.

The British sent a punitive force to Kabul on September 15, 1842. British General **George Pollock** ordered the citadel and great bazaar of the city burned, then departed with his army to India. The blow to British morale was heavy, and native tribesmen of Afganistan and other Third World countries gained the hope that the imperialist British forces were not invincible.

Fighting began in May 1846 when Mexican and American troops clashed along the **Rio Grande River**, which the United States claimed was the southern border of **Texas**--territory the United States had just annexed. Insisting that the **Neuces River** had always been the southern boundary, Mexico let itself be drawn into a war with its northern neighbor. When the fighting began, European observers predicted a Mexican victory, based on its larger standing army and longer military tradition. What those observers overlooked was the corruption that prevailed in the Mexican government and the relentless desire of Americans to fulfill what they believed to be their **Manifest Destiny**, the right to expand to the Pacific Ocean, regardless of any peoples--Indian, Spanish, Mexican, or other--who might stand in the way.

American General **Zachary Taylor (1784-**

General Winfield Scott

1850) won the two opening battles of the war and occupied the Mexican cities of **Matamoros** and **Monterrey**. At the same time, a spontaneous revolt occurred in **California**, which created the short-lived **Bear Flag Republic**, comprised of American adventurers who had been living under Mexican rule. Mexico continued to fight relentlessly, especially when **Antonio Lopez de Santa Anna (1795-1876)** again became president of the republic.

Santa Anna rushed a large army north from central Mexico to confront General Taylor at the **Battle of Buena Vista**. The battle was a bloody draw, and the Mexicans withdrew southward. Santa Anna returned with only half the men he had set out with, due to starvation, exposure and desertion. Meanwhile, American General **Winfield Scott (1786-1866)** arrived at **Veracruz** on the eastern coast of Mexico and took the city, after a superbly executed amphibious assault. Mexico still refused to accede to the American demands, and Scott took a small American army of 10,000 men to the Mexican interior, braving mountain passes, guerrilla fighters, and the unknown size of Santa Anna's army. Scott and his men arrived outside of Mexico City in early September and fought a series of battles. On September 14, 1847, American soldiers entered Mexico City in triumph. Santa Anna and the remainder of the resistance fled from the city.

Scott proved a model administrator, and peace negotiations that began in the fall led to the signing, in February 1848, of the **Treaty of Guadeloupe Hidalgo**, which gave the United States Texas, California, large sections of present-day Arizona, New Mexico, Colorado and Nevada. Mexico lost land, prestige and at least 30,000 soldiers during the war between the two North American republics.

64. REVOLUTIONS OF 1848-1849

Over an eighteen-month span in the middle of the nineteenth century, **Europeans** from France to Hungary rose against their rulers in a quest for greater personal freedom. Winning initial success, the **revolutionaries** encountered a severe reaction from conservative forces, and by mid-1849 nearly all the revolts had ended with a re-establishment of earlier regimes. The revolutionary movements showed that Europe was moving, slowly and painfully, toward an era of **liberalism** and **nationalism**.

Paris rose against the bourgeois monarchy of King **Louis Philippe (1773-1850)** on February 22, 1848. As the conservative Austrian statesman **Klemmens von Metternich** had observed in the past, "When France gets a cold, all of Europe sneezes." Louis Philippe soon went into exile, and the Parisians declared the establishment of the **Second Republic of France**. News of the French success spread to Austria and Prussia, where the king was forced to accede to a liberal constitution that called for a national assembly. Italian revolutionaries ousted Austrian troops from northern Italy, and Venice declared itself the new Venetian Republic. Poland, Hungary, Sweden and other European countries underwent similar changes. Only two major powers, Great Britain and Czarist Russia, were spared revolutionary uprisings in 1848, the former because it had a moderate, constitutional government already, the latter because of the repressive rule of Czar **Nicholas I (1796-1855)**.

In France, the people of the countryside resented the power of Paris in creating the Second Republic, and an army recruited from the villages defeated the radical demands of Parisians for the "right to work" (freedom from unemployment). The election of **Napoleon III (1808-1873)**, nephew of the former emperor, as President in December 1848 signaled the end of revolutionary sentiment in France for the time being.

In Austria, the king used artillery to bombard the city of Vienna and subdue the people who had forced him to change his government earlier in the year. Helpless to control the revolutionary movement in Hungary, the Austrian government asked the help of Czar Nicolas I, often called the "gendarme of Europe." The Czar sent 200,000 soldiers, who defeated the Hungarians and returned the province to Austrian control. Perhaps the greatest disappointments were in Germany and Italy, two countries that had not been unified since the Middle Ages. King **Frederick William IV** disbanded the **National Assembly**, which had sought to create a unified Germany under the leadership of Prussia, and Italy found itself returned to Austrian control by the means of French troops, sent by the new President Napoleon III, to reestablish order in Rome. Austria soon regained its control of northern Italy, bringing the revolutionary movement to a close.

Monumental as were the failures of 1848, they showed the disposition of the European people toward liberalism and nationalism.

King Louis Philippe

65. TAIPING REBELLION
1850-1864

Battle of the Taiping Rebellion

The Manchu government of China had hardly recovered from the effects of the **First Opium War** (see no. 61), when it was faced with an internal disturbance in 1850. The imperial government in Peking sent units of the Chinese army to break up a new religious sect that was based, in part, on Protestant doctrine. Led by the scholar **Hung His-ch'uan**, the followers of the new movement defeated the army forces sent against them, and what had begun as an iconoclastic revolt magnified into a full-scale civil war.

Gathering large numbers of followers, His-ch'uan overran the government defenses in the Yangtze river provinces. Lacking military supplies, the rebels captured a government arsenal at Yochow, then proceeded down the Yangtze Valley and captured **Nanking**, where His-ch'uan proclaimed his own new dynasty, the **Taiping**, or "Great Peace."

The Taiping rebels announced their intention to reject China's **Confucian** heritage and institute land reforms that would create something like a communal society (this was only a few years after the word "Communist" had first been used by Karl Marx in the *Communist Manifesto*). The Manchu government was at first helpless, but as the goals of the rebel leaders were announced, the majority of China's bureaucrats and scholars--alarmed by the rejection of Confucianism--turned solidly against the rebels, who did not manage to penetrate further north after 1853. A stalemate developed that lasted for seven years, with the Manchu government holding North China and the Taiping rebels controlling the south.

In 1860, as the **Second Opium War** (see no. 67) came to an end, the victorious European powers decided it was in their best interest to assist the Manchu government. European ships patrolled the waters of southern China and prevented coastal movements by the rebels. **Frederick Townshend Ward (1831-1862)**, an American sailing captain from Salem, Massachusetts, formed and commanded a small 4,000-man army equipped with Western-style weapons. His victories over the rebels led to his group being called the "Ever-Victorious Army." Following his death, he was replaced by a British officer, **Charles George "Chinese" Gordon**. Ward and Gordon's efforts resulted in many of the walled cities on the coast of southern China surrendering to the government forces. Nanking was taken by storm in July 1864, and the last resistance was overwhelmed in 1865.

The war had cost millions of Chinese lives and large parts of China lay in ruins. Taken together with the First and Second Opium wars, the Taiping rebellion demonstrated both the weakness of the Manchu dynasty and the vulnerability of imperial China to outside influence, especially from European powers.

In 1853, a war began between countries located at the far ends of Europe, nearly a thousand miles apart from each other. Czar **Nicholas I (1796-1855)** of Russia claimed that Russia had the right to protect the religious freedom of the **Orthodox Christians** who lived within the boundaries of the **Ottoman Empire**. The Turkish rulers in Constantinople rejected this claim. Russian troops then moved to occupy the provinces of **Moldavia** and **Wallachia**, on the western side of the Black Sea.

The Battle of Balaklava

The Ottomans declared war on Russia, but the Russians made the first military move, sending their fleet against the Turkish ships on November 30, 1853. The Russians won the **Battle of Sinop** and seemed well on their way to gaining land and other concessions from the ailing Ottoman Empire, which by this time was often referred to as the "sick old man of Europe."

Britain and France did not wish to see Russian ships in the Mediterranean, so they sent a joint naval force to the Black Sea, ordering the Russians to return their ships to port. When the Russians refused, Queen **Victoria (1819-1901)** of England and **Napoleon III (1808-1873)** of France declared war on Russia. Czar Nicholas I hoped for help from Austria or Prussia, but both countries remained neutral, leaving Russia to battle it out alone.

In September 1854, a joint force of British, French, Turkish, and Sardinian troops landed on the **Crimean Peninsula** in southern Russia. They commenced what turned into a year-long siege of the fortified city and naval base of **Sevastopol** from September 28, 1854 to September 8, 1855. During the siege, the

French and British won the **Battle of Balaklava**, immortalized in Tennyson's poem, "The Charge of the Light Brigade". The Russians fought with great courage, but their supply system--composed of ox carts dragging supplies hundreds of miles from Moscow--could not compete with the water-borne transport of the British, French and their allies. In defeat, the Russians blew up large sections of the Sevastopol fortress and evacuated the city. The **Congress of Paris** in 1856 laid out the peace terms: the Ottoman Empire maintained its territorial integrity, Russia was given no role regarding Orthodox Christians in the Ottoman lands, and the self-governing status of Moldavia and Wallachia was protected.

The war saw the advent of important new technical developments. The news camera, telegraph and steel-hulled ship were used for the first time in warfare. **Florence Nightingale (1820-1910)** served as a nurse in the war and, inspired by the horrendous hospital conditions she witnessed, began her campaign for improvements in medical treatment for soldiers.

The essential dilemma that faced Imperial China in 1856, was whether she should allow expansion of the trade privileges that Western nations had gained as a result of the **First Opium War** (see no. 61). The Manchu government of China was beleaguered by the **Taiping Rebellion** (see no. 65) within its own borders; at the same time, British and French diplomats were putting pressure on China to open themselves even more to contact with the West.

In 1856, the Chinese seized the **Arrow**, a Chinese-owned vessel flying the British Union Jack, which was engaged in the illegal trade of opium. Using this incident as a pretext, the British and French governments sent a joint force that took and occupied the port city of **Canton** in southern China in 1857. The European fleet then sailed north, captured, and briefly held the **Taku forts** near the city of **Tientsin**.

Responding to these threats, and to the continuing menace presented by the Taiping Rebellion, the Chinese government signed the **Treaties of Tientsin** with Britain, France, Russia, and the United States in June 1858. Under the treaties, China opened more of its ports to foreign trade, allowed foreign diplomats to reside in the city of Peking, and legalized the importation of opium. These were humiliating concessions for a country as proud as Manchu China to make.

Soon after the treaties were signed, foreign diplomats were refused entrance to Peking, and an invading British force was slaughtered by the Chinese near Tientsin. The British and French seized the Taku forts for a second time, moved upriver, and captured Tientsin itself. In 1860, the British and French defeated a Chinese army outside of Peking; the Chinese emperor fled, and for the first time in the memory of any Chinese historian, foreign armies entered the capital city.

A group of Chinese commissioners, negotiating for the emperor, concluded four new treaties with the Europeans. The Chinese opened more ports to foreign trade, and gave British, French, Russian, and American diplomats the right to live in Peking. The war essentially opened the entire Chinese empire to influence from the West; a bargain for the beleaguered Manchu government which was, at the same time, fighting for its life against the Taiping Rebellion, threatening the fabric of China itself.

The Battle of Pa-Li-Kao

Great Britain had dominated the economy of India since the **Battle of Plassey** in 1757, but it was not until the great rebellion of 1857 to 1858 that Britain came to govern India officially. **The British East India Company** (the same company that had suffered from the Boston Tea Party and transported opium to China prior to the **First Opium War**) had great influence in India, but it governed the territory it controlled as a mercantile concern, not as part of the British empire.

In 1856, the company annexed the Indian state of **Oudh**, one of the worst-governed of the Indian principalities, but the one from which most of the **sepoys** (native soldiers serving the company) were recruited. On May 10, 1857, the soldiers of the Benghal army at **Meerut** in northern India rebelled against their British officers. Long and detailed studies of the revolt indicate that it came about due to the sepoy's belief that the cartridges being issued with the new **Enfield rifles** were greased with animal fat, something that was not only deeply offensive, but actually taboo, to both Hindus and Muslims.

The mutiny at Meerut soon inspired other soldiers to revolt; northern India became a battleground between Englishmen and native Indians. The sepoys captured the key city of **Delhi** and named the aged Mogul emperor as their leader. The rebels then seized

Lucknow and **Kanpur**, and the British temporarily lost control of the Ganges heartland, as well as parts of the Punjab and Deccan. While southern India remained calm, northern and central India were rife with rural rebellions and guerrilla actions, carried out with ferocity on both sides.

The mutiny was suppressed with severity by the British. Vivid moments of the war, such as the blowing up of the powder magazine at Delhi, the siege of Cawnpore, and the British relief of the city of Lucknow, became legendary to the British in India who grew up in the war's aftermath.

The war left great bitterness among the Indians and led to a posture of aloofness and superiority on the part of the British. **The Government of India Act** of 1858 transferred authority for the administration of the subcontinent from the East India Company to the British crown and provided for the creation of a secretary of state in the British cabinet with full responsibility for India.

Attack on the Alambagh

Italy had not been politically united since the time of the Roman Empire. As late as 1848, Italy was still divided into the feudal divisions of the **Kingdom of Sardinia**, the **Dukedom of Milan**, the **Papal States**, and the **Kingdom of the Two Sicilies**. Then, as now, the northern part of Italy was more prosperous than the southern, and the impetus toward unification came from the north, where two very different men called for Italian unification: **Camillo Benso, Count of Cavour (1810-1861)** and **Giuseppe Garibaldi (1807-1882)**, the adventurer.

Cavour was Prime Minister of the Kingdom of Sardinia. He conspired with French Emperor **Napoleon III (1808-1873)** to fight jointly against the Austrians, who had for so long held a dominant hand in the politics and affairs of northern Italy. In the short war that followed, the French weaponry proved decisive, though the casualties were costly for both sides. Austria was exiled from northern Italy, and Cavour was able to report to King **Victor Emmanuel** of Sardinia that northern Italy was willing to follow his leadership.

Cavour was a practical nationalist; he yearned to modernize and industrialize his country. His unlikely counterpart was Garibaldi, a romantic nationalist who had spent most of his life fighting for freedom, whether in Italy or Central or South America. The failure of the **Revolutions of 1848** to bring about Italian unification had discouraged Garibaldi, but he returned to his homeland in 1859, and in the following year led his famed **Red Shirts** to the island of Sicily.

Garibaldi's 1,000 volunteers were loosely organized and poorly armed, but they brought with them an indomitable spirit and determination. Landing in Sicily, they managed to win the good will of the local population, and in six weeks they routed the 25,000-man army of the Neapolitan rulers. Crossing into the toe of the boot of Italy, Garibaldi's men began marching north; on their way they were met by Cavour and King Victor Emmanuel, who had ridden south to take advantage of the momentum established by Garibaldi's success.

Meeting the king and prime minister on the road south of Naples, Garibaldi gracefully yielded his conquests and new sovereignty to the king. Receiving little recompense for his efforts, Garibaldi stepped off the stage of world history just as he reached the acme of his success. Few other examples of selfless patriotism can compare to that of Garibaldi's, and his name was revered by the romantic nationalists of the nineteenth century. Italy was unified in 1860.

Giuseppe Garibaldi

By 1860, just prior to the start of the **Civil War**, American frontiersmen and settlers had reached the edge of the Great Plains. The landscapes of states such as Montana, the Dakotas, Colorado and Kansas show little evidence of the Indian communities that once thrived there. Tribes such as the **Cheyenne, Sioux, Apache, Navajo**, and **Comanche** had developed a relationship with the land and its resources. They used horses that had come to them wild (descendants of the horses brought to the Americas by the Spanish conquistadores) to traverse the great distances of the American West.

Sitting Bull

Wars began as soon as settlers encroached on the territorial lands of these tribes. The **Apache and Navajo War** of 1860 to 1865 took place simultaneously with the Civil War, and the **Sioux War** of 1862 to 1864 showed the determination of the Sioux to fight for their lands in Minnesota. The **Cheyenne and Apache War** of 1864 to 1868 began after the U.S. Army destroyed the winter camp of the Cheyennes. Tribes, from Colorado to Texas, rose against the encroachers. Three US Army columns were dispatched in 1865, which wiped out one Arapaho camp, and the war soon fizzled to a close.

Red Cloud's War from 1866 to 1869 and the **Red River War** from 1874 to 1875 showed the destructive power of the United States Army. Civil War hero **William Tecumseh Sherman (1820-1891)** declared an all-out war on the tribes in northern Texas in 1874 and proceeded to fight fourteen

pitched battles against them. Most of the Indians returned to their reservations by 1875. When the Comanches yielded, there were hardly any free Indians left on the southern plains.

The **Sioux War** of 1876 to 1877 was provoked by the discovery of gold in the Black Hills of South Dakota, and a rush of white settlers to that area. The Army troops were led by generals **George Crook** and **Alfred H. Terry**, but it was the annihilation of a detachment of men, led by Colonel **George Armstrong Custer (1839-1876)**, that sparked interest in the American public. The Indian victory at **Little Big Horn** was short-lived; **Chief Crazy Horse (1842-1877)** surrendered the next year, and **Chief Sitting Bull (1831-1890)** escaped to Canada.

The **Nez Pearce War** of 1877 was another setback for the Native Americans. Finding he could not defeat the U.S. Army, **Chief Joseph** led his tribe on a 1,500-mile march through difficult country, trying to reach the safety of the Canadian border. Caught only forty miles away from Canada, Chief Joseph and his people surrendered on October 5, 1877.

The final U.S. Army-American Indian war came in 1890, when the power of the tribes was greatly diminished. The Sioux were practicing a ritual called the **Ghost Dances** that led to visions, trances and group frenzy. The U.S. government decided this was dangerous and sent forth the Seventh Cavalry, which fought and defeated the Sioux on the Black Hills reservation at **Wounded Knee** in South Dakota on December 29, 1890.

General William Tecumseh Sherman

The names of **Robert E. Lee, (1807-1870) Ulysses Simpson Grant (1822-1885)** and **Thomas J. "Stonewall" Jackson: (1824-1863)** bring to mind the passion and glory of the **American Civil War**.

The war began in April 1861, when **Confederate** soldiers fired on **Fort Sumter** in the harbor of Charleston, South Carolina. The eleven states of the Confederacy soon came together to resist the subsequent invasions by **Union** soldiers from the northern states, whose commander-in-chief was the newly elected President **Abraham Lincoln (1809-1865)**. The war was fought over two main issues: union or secession and slavery or freedom.

The North had a larger population, greater industrial capacity, and a larger share of the nation's wealth. Southerners counted on a longer military tradition, and the importance of cotton to European countries such as Britain and France; they expected those countries to ally with them in their bid for freedom from the Union.

The first battles of the war generally went to the Confederates, who won the **Battle of Bull Run**, and defended Virginia from a large Union invasion in the **Battle of Seven Days**. Union General Ulysses S. Grant captured two key Confederate forts, and fought the Southerners to a draw at the bloody **Battle of Shiloh**.

Knowing that the North would eventually prevail through sheer weight of numbers, Confederate General Robert E. Lee led two invasions of the North that resulted in the titanic battles of **Antietam** in 1862 and **Gettysburg** in 1863. Antietam was a bloody draw: the Confederacy did not succeed in winning on northern soil, nor did the Union pursue Lee's retreating army. A week later Lincoln published the **Emancipation Proclamation**, freeing all slaves in territory not yet conquered by the Union army. The battle at Gettysburg broke the back of Lee's offensive power. President Lincoln brought General Grant from the west and commanded him to go after Lee.

Following a series of bloody battles in northern Virginia, Grant commanded a long siege of the twin cities of **Richmond** and **Petersburg**, Virginia during the winter of 1864 to 1865. Meanwhile, General **William Tecumseh Sherman (1820-1891)** led the Union armies of the west into **Atlanta**, and then made a march through the south that fulfilled his promise to "make Georgia howl."

Lee attempted to break out of the siege of Richmond and Petersburg in April 1865. He was surrounded and trapped by Grant's men and he surrendered at **Appomattox Courthouse**. The last remaining Confederate army surrendered near Durham, North Carolina to Sherman's army.

President Lincoln was killed by the bullet of **James Wilkes Booth** just as the war was coming to an end. The war made the United States truly one indivisible nation. Over 600,000 men had been killed or wounded.

FRENCH INTERVENTION IN MEXICO
1862-1867

In 1861, Mexican President **Benito Juarez (1806-1872)** declared a moratorium on all the country's foreign debts. The country had endured a rocky start in the nineteenth century (see no. 57, no. 60 and no. 63), and Juarez wanted to buy time for his people to regain economic stability. Unfortunately, Britain, France and Spain, three of the main debtor nations, signed the **Convention of London** in October 1861, committing those countries to a program of recovering their debts from Mexico.

A joint expedition of British, French and Spanish troops occupied **Vera Cruz**, on the eastern coast of Mexico in 1862. The British and Spanish withdrew their forces after conferring with Mexican leaders about potential debt payments, but **Napoleon III (1808-1873)**, emperor of France, dreamed of creating a new French empire in Middle America.

French troops advanced into Mexico, but were defeated at **Puebla** by a Mexican army led by **Ignacio Zaragoza**. Napoleon III sent more soldiers across the ocean and French General **Elie Frederic Forey** captured Puebla after a two months' siege in May 1863. The French continued on and entered **Mexico City** on June 7, 1863. French General **Achille Bazaine** moved west from Mexico City, entering and occupying Mexican cities without resistance, while President Juarez fled to the north and established a government in exile, near the Mexican border with Texas.

In 1864, Napoleon III sent Austrian Archduke **Ferdinand Maximilian (1832-1867)** to Mexico and had him installed as a puppet emperor. Napoleon promised French military support for the next three years on condition that Maximilian seek to collect the monies owed to France. Some conservative Mexicans, weary of years of revolution and war, welcomed the appearance of Maximilian and supported his new government.

In 1865, General **Philip Sheridan** advanced with American troops as far as the **Rio Grande River**, while the U.S. government made official diplomatic protests over the French presence in Mexico. At the same time, guerilla armies formed in southern Mexico.

The execution of Ferdinand Maximilian

Beset on all sides, Maximilian lost his main support when Napoleon III began to withdraw his troops at the end of 1866. Maximilian was betrayed, courtmartialed, and executed on June 19, 1867, ending both his personal bid for glory and the last French imperial presence in the New World.

AUSTRO-PRUSSIAN WAR
1866

In 1866, the still-disunited **Germany** faced a momentous question: would **Austria** or **Prussia** dominate the future of central Europe? From the time of **Napoleon Bonaparte's (1769-1821)** defeat in 1815, Austria had exerted a powerful influence over the **German Confederation**; during the heyday of Austria Prime Minister **Klemmens von Metternich**, Austrian policemen and spies had infiltrated the confederation, trying to root out support for liberalism and nationalism, notions that the Napoleonic era had promoted.

In 1862, **Otto von Bismarck (1815-1898)** became Chancellor of the **Kingdom of Prussia** Bismarck made clear his determination in a famous speech on September 29, 1862: "The great questions of the day will not be settled by means of speeches and majority decisions...but by iron and blood." The great question of the day, of

Otto von Bismarck

course, was whether Germany would be united, and if so, under Austrian or Prussian influence.

Bismarck persuaded a somewhat reluctant King **Wilhelm I** of Prussia to significantly increase the size of the army. Bismarck studied the lessons of the **Crimean War** (see no.66) and determined that planning, transportation, and communication were the keys to success in war during the nineteenth century. He developed the Prussian General Staff, composed of the best and brightest of his military men, to plan in exact detail all the campaigns

of a war. Bismarck also increased the number of railroad and telegraph lines from Berlin to all military locations in the country.

He then provoked Austria into declaring war on Prussia by occupying the **Duchy of Holstein**, which had been administered by Austria for the previous two years. The **Habsburg** monarchy in Vienna went into the war confidently, little realizing the advances in transportation and communications that had been effected in Prussia.

The **Austro-Prussian War**, also called the **Seven Weeks' War**, culminated at the **Battle of Sadowa** (Koniggratz) in eastern Bohemia on July 3, 1866. The battle was a seesaw affair, and Bismarck, fed continual information by telegraph, briefly considered suicide as the day threatened to get out of hand. Instead, Prussian reinforcements reached the battle by speedy trains, and Prussia won a crucial victory. Austria bowed out of the war quickly, and the **Treaty of Prague**, signed on August 23, 1866 excluded Austria from involvement in the affairs of the German Confederation, which was renamed the German Confederation of the North. Prussia gained direct control of Schleswig-Holstein, Hanover, Hesse, and Frankfurt. Bismarck had already achieved more than any other Prussian leader to date, but he soon cast his eye on another potential rival: the France of **Napoleon III.**

In 1870, a crisis developed when two rival countries emerged to claim the throne of Spain. Both France and Prussia had some substance to their claims, but France was alarmed by the prospect of being bracketed by Prussia on one side and Spain on the other, both ruled by the same monarch. The French ambassador to Prussia visited King **Wilhelm I** of Prussia at his retreat at Ems, where he was taking the waters. Refusing to absolutely rule out his family as a possible contender for the Spanish throne, the king sent the ambassador away. Chancellor of Prussia, **Otto von Bismarck (1815-1898)**, cleverly edited the news telegram of the event to make it seem as if the king had been deliberately rude to the ambassador. When the French public read the "Ems Dispatch," the people were incensed, and cries of "War" and "On to Berlin" were heard. Bismarck's manipulations led **Napoleon III (1803-1873)** to declare war on Prussia on July 19, 1871, a war for which the French were unprepared.

Three Prussian armies invaded France almost at once, and French General **Achille Bazaine** led an army eastward to meet the Prussians. His men defended themselves ably at the **Battle of Gravelotte** on August 18, but the French failed to counterattack, and Bazaine led his forces to refuge in the fortress city of **Metz**. One Prussian army pursued Bazaine, and carried out a 54-day siege, which ended with the surrender of Bazaine's entire army.

Meanwhile, on September 1, 1871, the largest section of the French army, with Napoleon III in command, was defeated at the **Battle of Sedan**. Napoleon surrendered himself and 80,000 men the following day.

Despite the capture of the emperor, France fought bravely on. A provisional government

The French surrender at Metz

was set up in Paris; it quickly deposed Napoleon III, declared the creation of the **Third French Republic**, and prepared to defend Paris. Two Prussian armies besieged the French capital from September 19, 1870 through January 28, 1871, when the city finally surrendered due to famine.

Meanwhile, on January 18, 1871, Bismarck and King Wilhelm I of Prussia had declared that Prussia would head a new, united Germany. The **German Empire** was formally proclaimed in the **Hall of Mirrors** at Versailles. King Wilhelm I became German Emperor and Bismarck remained in his position as chancellor. Bismarck had worked a diplomatic miracle in bringing four kingdoms (Prussia, Bavaria, Saxony, Wuttenberg), five grand duchies, thirteen duchies, and three free cities (Bremen, Hamburg, Lubeck) together to form the first united Germany since the early period of the Holy Roman Empire in the twelfth century.

The **Treaty of Frankfurt** signed on May 10, 1871 allowed Germany to take and hold the former French provinces of Alsace and Lorraine, and for France to pay an indemnity of five billion francs (around one billion dollars).

SECOND AFGHAN WAR
1878-1880

Tensions between Russia and Great Britain led to the outbreak of the **Second Afghan War** in 1878. **Sher Ali** had succeeded his father, **Dost Mohammed**, as emir of Afghanistan in 1863. Russia moved soldiers close to the border with Afghanistan in 1878 and dispatched a diplomatic mission to Sher Ali. The British in India hastened to do the same, but the British diplomats were stopped by Afghan border guards at the **Khyber Pass**. The British demanded an apology and explanation from Sher Ali; unsatisfied with his response, they invaded from the south.

As the British troops entered his country in November 1878, Sher Ali fled to the north and asked the Russians for help. Advised by the Russians to return and make peace with the British, he declined to do so, and died shortly afterward in Mazar-i-Sharif. Sher Ali's son, **Yakub Khan**, concluded a treaty yielding control of the Khyber Pass and other strategic points to the British. However, the invaders made the same mistake committed in 1839 (see no. 62), believing that the emir had as much power as a king, when he was in fact regarded as first among equals of Afghani tribal leaders.

Yakub Khan

British representatives sent to Kabul in 1879 were murdered by Afghanis who resented the notion that their country's foreign policy should be dictated from London. Furious over this breach of treaty, the British sent three armies northward. They captured Kabul and Kandahar, and Yakub Khan went into exile. Twelve different Afghan tribes soon made war on the British invaders with a new leader in command, **Sirdar Abdur Rahman**, a grandson of Dost Mohammed and cousin of Yakub Khan. He had been in exile in Russia for 12 years, but when he appeared on the Oxus River in northern Afghanistan, the tribes rallied to him. As he advanced to Kabul, the British withdrew from the city. Sirdar Abdur Rahman proved to be someone that both the Afghans and the British could live with as the new leader. He did much to diminish the power of the different tribes and integrated most of Afghanistan into a single political unit. In 1893, his talks with the British resulted in the drawing of the **Durand Line**, which still forms the border between Afghanistan and Pakistan today.

In 1879, soldiers of the British Victorian army encountered the most fearless, reckless and unusual fighters of any they had battled during the nineteenth century: warriors of the **Zulu** tribe of southern Africa.

The Zulu nation had been founded in 1816 by the chief **Shaka**, who had persuaded his warriors to abandon their traditional weapon --the throwing javelin--and take up the stabbing spear instead. Zulu warriors had fought against the **Dutch Boers** in 1838 and been defeated at the **Battle of Blood River**. Following the loss, the Zulus returned to their area, called **Zululand**, and lived there as the dominant tribe in their region for 40 years. The British annexed the **Transvaal** area in 1877 and inherited what some would call the "Zulu problem" from the Boers.

Arrogant due to their long history of success in fighting against native tribesmen, the British demanded de facto control over Zululand. Zulu King **Cetewayo** ignored the demand, and British General **Frederic Thesiger** invaded Zululand with three columns of British troops and native allies in early January 1879.

The first battle was fought at **Isandlwana**, where thousands of Zulus surrounded a detachment of British troops. When other British soldiers arrived a day later they found the bodies of 52 British officers and 806 enlisted men, as well as 500 native allies on the field. The victorious Zulus, who had overwhelmed the British with their attacks, had paid for the victory with roughly 3,000 men killed.

Zulu and British bravery were again demonstrated on January 22 to 23, 1879, when 4,000 Zulus attacked 140 British soldiers, equipped with rifles and artillery. The Zulus left 1,000 men dead after a series of attacks that lasted 10 hours and resulted in the awarding of more Victoria's crosses (medals of valor) than any other British battle before or since. Reinforcements for the British army arrived in April and May. One of the soldiers who came was the Prince Imperial of Napoleonic France, **Louis J.J. Bonaparte**, son of the former **Napoleon III**. The prince's death, from a Zulu spear, on June 2, 1879 made the war appear even more savage to Europeans, who read vivid newspaper stories about the wild bravery of the Zulus and the indomitable spirit of the British.

The Zulus put up strong resistance at the battles of **Esghowe** and **Kambula**, but were defeated at **Ulandi** on July 4. King Cetewayo escaped the battlefield, but was captured in August and made to seek peace terms with the British. Great Britain officially annexed Zululand in 1887. Some 10,000 Zulus were killed in the war; the British lost 1,100 men and expended $5 million in the prosecution of the war.

King Cetewayo

Ninety miles from the Florida coast, **Cuba** has long been of interest to the continental United States. In 1962, President **John F. Kennedy (1917-1963)** nearly committed the United States to war with Russia over missiles placed on the island. The American desire to control events in Cuba dates as far back as the 1850s, when reckless American free agents attempted to seize control. True American takeover occurred in 1898, when the young and brash United States confronted an aging imperial Spain for mastery of the Caribbean and the Philippines.

Spain tried to put down insurrections in its colonial possessions of Cuba and the **Philippines** during the 1890s. American newspapers, led by publisher **William Randolph Hearst**, trumpeted atrocities that were committed by the Spaniards and called on all red-blooded Americans to end Spanish control in the Western hemisphere. It took the explosion of the battleship **USS Maine**, anchored in Havana, on February 1, 1898, to bring a majority of Americans into line with the views expressed in the newspaper columns. It was not then--nor has it ever been since--proved that the ship was blown up by Spaniards, but public intemperance overrode scruples, and by mid-spring the United States was at war with Spain.

It was a curious mismatch, pitting a country with a decrepit fleet against a young imperial power that had just finished building the fifth best steel navy in the world. On May 1, 1898, American Commodore **George Dewey** entered the harbor in **Manila Bay** and soon destroyed the Spanish fleet anchored there; Dewey lost only one man in the battle. Elsewhere, American troops arrived in the Philippines, where they were received as liberators by the Filipinos.

The going was harder in the Caribbean, where large numbers of Americans were recruited to fight. The Americans went by ship from Florida to Cuba, where they began a long campaign of pushing the Spaniards back to **Santiago**. Yellow fever and dysentery were formidable foes for the Americans, and the fighting proved more difficult than had been expected. On July 1, 1898, Colonel **Theodore Roosevelt (1858-1919)** and his **Rough Riders** (a strange combination of Ivy League students and cowboys) captured **Kettle Hill** (usually misnamed San Juan Hill), breaking the center of the Spanish positions around Santiago. When the Americans pressed closer to the city, the Spanish admiral tried to escape with his fleet. The ensuing naval battle was nearly as one-sided as the battle of Manila had been; the Spanish fleet was destroyed, and the United States became unquestionably the number one naval power in the Caribbean Sea.

Under the terms of the peace treaty, the United States received **Puerto Rico** and the Philippines from Spain. It established a protectorate over Cuba, and soon, under the new presidential leadership of none other than Theodore Roosevelt, was on its way to building the **Panama Canal** that would unite the Caribbean with the Pacific Ocean.

The USS Maine in Havanna Harbor

The first Europeans to erect a permanent settlement in Africa were **Dutch Calvinists** who arrived at Capetown in 1652. Over the next two hundred years, they evolved into a distinct ethnic group known as the **Boers**. Even though the Netherlands lost its territory in South Africa to the British around 1800, the Boers kept their identity and moved hundreds of miles inland, during the famous **Boer Trek** of 1835 to 1837 to escape British rule.

Great Britain formally annexed the **Transvaal** (Boer state) in 1877; the Boers responded by proclaiming a new **South African Republic**. Determined fighters, the Boers repulsed the British at **Laing's Neck** and **Ingogo** and inflicted a major defeat upon their enemies at **Majuba Hill** on February 28, 1881. **The Convention of Pretoria** gave internal independence to the Boers, but conceded a vague British "suzerainty" over the foreign affairs of the South African Republic.

The second or **Great Boer War** began in 1899. Gold had been discovered in the Transvaal and the rush of foreigners greatly offended the Boers. British troops entered the Transvaal, ostensibly to protect British mining interests. The Boers gave them a deadline for departure; when they failed to observe the date, the South African Republic and its ally, the **Orange Free State**, declared war on Great Britain on October 11, 1899.

Many Englishmen thought the war would be a walkover, a splendid end to a century in which British arms had triumphed everywhere from **Waterloo** and **Trafalgar** to the **Zulu War** (see no. 76). Instead, the British were rocked back on their heels by the aggressive Boer tactics; Boer forces led by men such as **Piet Conje, Louis Botha**, and **Jacobus De La Rey** captured the cities of Kimberly, Mafeking, and Ladysmith. Conje won the **Battle of Magersfontein** on December 10 to 11, 1899 and Botha defeated British General **Redvers Buller** at the **Battle of Colenso** on December 15, 1899

The British struck back in 1900. Large numbers of fresh troops arrived in South Africa, and under the leadership of **Lord Frederick Roberts** and **Lord Horatio Kitchener** began the long marches that culminated in the capture of Johannesburg on May 31 and Pretoria on June 5, 1900. Roberts soon left for England, but Kitchener remained to fight a two-year war against the Boers' guerrilla forces. Kitchener built a series of blockhouses to divide the country, and erected concentration camps where some estimate 18,000 to 28,000 Boer men, women and children died.

The Treaty of Vereeniging of May 31, 1902 ended the war. The Boers accepted British sovereignty, but they received in return a large war indemnity and other concessions that led many English people to say that the Boers had lost the war, but won the peace. Britain placed a total of 365,000 imperial troops and 82,000 colonial soldiers in the field and spent 200 million pounds. At least 22,000 British, 25,000 Boers, and 12,000 Africans died.

Boers prepared for battle

President Theodore Roosevelt as peace maker

Few foreign observers expected much development in nineteenth century Japan, making her victory in the **Russo-Japanese War** even more remarkable. Japan had been "opened" to Western influence in 1853 by the appearance of American steamships. From 1870 on, the island nation underwent a fast process of industrialization and modernization of its armed forces.

In 1904, Japan tried to persuade Czarist Russia to agree to a mutual recognition of Japanese and Russian interests in **Manchuria** and **Korea**. The Russians negotiated in a dilatory fashion, and on February 6, 1904, the Japanese ambassador abruptly broke off the talks and went home. Two days later, the Japanese fleet sank two Russian warships at **Chemulpo**, Korea and made a torpedo boat attack on the main Russian fleet anchored at **Port Arthur** on the Liaotung peninsula (which Russia had leased from Imperial China).

The rest of the Russian ships were anchored at **Vladivostok** to the north, frozen in by ice.

Given its sudden superiority at sea, the Japanese Navy was able to bring hundreds of thousands of troops to the Asian mainland and attack the Russian posts there. The Japanese overran Korea quickly, and by May 1 they were in Manchuria. By September, the Russian army had been pushed north to Mukden, and Port Arthur was surrounded by both land and sea. Two bloody, but indecisive battles, were fought near Mukden, and the Japanese settled down to a long siege of Port Arthur.

Using machine guns, the Russians were aggressive toward the Japanese forces, but on January 2, 1905, Port Arthur was forced to surrender. After the deadly **Battle of Mukden** on February 21 to March 10, 1905, the Japanese claimed victory, but the casualties were so great on both sides, that neither side truly won.

By mid 1905, both Japan and Russia were weary of war. At that time the Russian Baltic Fleet had finally arrived in the Pacific, having sailed halfway around the world. Steaming toward Vladivostok, the Baltic Fleet was met by the Japanese Imperial Fleet on May 27 to 28 at the naval **Battle of Tsushima Straits**. The Japanese won an overwhelming victory, capturing the entire Russian fleet while losing only three torpedo boats themselves.

Accepting the offer of American President **Theodore Roosevelt (1858-1919)** to act as a mediator, Russian and Japanese representatives met at Portsmouth, New Hampshire on August 10, 1905. The **Treaty of Portsmouth**, signed September 5, 1905, gave the southern half of Sakhalin Island to Japan. Russia recognized Japanese interests in Korea, and transferred the land it had leased from China on the Liaotung peninsula, to Japan, as well as granting them fishing rights off the coast of Siberia. It was a tremendous gain for Japan, which had vaulted into prominence as the only Asian country of its time period that was able to defeat a major European power.

By 1912, festering resentments in the **Balkans** had created a situation that was ready to explode. The long-standing **Ottoman** domination of the area could not continue. Encouraged by Czarist **Russia**, which considered itself the protector of the Slavic peoples, Greece, Serbia, Bulgaria, and Montenegro formed the **Balkan League** in 1912. Arguing that their Slavic cousins who lived within the boundaries of the Ottoman Empire were being mistreated, the countries demanded that the Ottomans reform their rule.

The Ottoman sultan hesitated to make changes, and the **First Balkan War** began in 1912. The Greeks trapped a Turkish army and liberated Salonika, while the Serbs moved south and won the battles of **Kumanovov** and **Montastir** in the fall of 1912. Invading the Ottoman domain from the east, Bulgarian forces won the battles of **Kirk Kilissa** and **Lule Burgas**, where they engaged the main Turkish army and sent it in full retreat toward **Constantinople**. Supply problems prevented the Bulgarians from taking **Adrianople** and Constantinople. A Turkish-Bulgarian armistice was agreed to on December 3, 1912.

Enraged by this display of weakness in the field, the "Young Turks," a group of army officers, ousted the sultan and set up a new Ottoman government. They renewed the war, but suffered yet another loss, when Adrianople fell to Bulgarian and Serbian troops on March 3, 1913. The Ottomans accepted the terms of the **Treaty of London**, under which they lost Crete and half their land in Europe.

The **Second Balkan War** in 1913 broke out when the "Young Turks" rejected the peace terms of the Treaty of London. The Turks were in luck, since the victors of the First Balkan War had fallen out among themselves. Bulgaria went to war with Serbia in June 1913, and by July, Serb and Greek forces had checked the Bulgarians, who were soon attacked by the Romanians as well. Given all this confusion, it is not surprising that the Turks were able to recapture Adrianople on July 20, 1913. The **Treaty of Bucharest** of August 10, 1913 ceded all the territory Bulgaria had won in the First Balkan War to her former allies, Serbia, Greece and Montenegro. The Ottoman leaders retained Adrianople, but the combination of the two wars had greatly reduced Turkish influence in Europe.

Few students of history dispute the three major causes of **World War I**: nationalism (especially in the Balkans), a build-up of arms since 1890, and entangling alliances.

In August 1914, **Archduke Ferdinand**, heir to the throne of Austria-Hungary, was shot down in **Sarajevo**. His death set off a chain of events that soon led to the German Empire, Austria-Hungary and the Ottoman Empire (present-day Turkey) facing off against a combination of powers that included Britain, France, Russia, and eventually the United States.

Germany began the war with an all-out effort to crush France, so it could concentrate its forces against Russia in the east. Failing to take Paris in 1914, Germany settled into a long four years of trench warfare on the western front. German, French and British soldiers became accustomed to hearing "Over the top!"--the signal for them to come out from their trenches and charge across the "No-Man's Land" of barbed wire and explosives to try to reach the enemy's lines. The combination of machine-gun fire and gun emplacements made offensive movement nearly impossible, and the three countries settled into deadly battles of attrition such as

German soldiers in trenches

Verdun and the **Somme**. The fighting on the eastern front was more fluid; Russian armies usually defeated the Austrians, but then found themselves pushed back by the German forces.

In an effort to break the deadlock, Britain tried to open the Dardanelles and capture Constantinople; the result was the **Gallipoli** campaign which cost the Allies a quarter of a million casualties. The two events that broke the deadlock were the **Russian Revolution** and the entry of the United States into the war. The Americans reluctantly entered because of submarine warfare that sank a number of passenger ships carrying American citizens; in April 1917, President **Woodrow Wilson (1856-1924)** vowed to make the world safe for democracy, and a million American doughboys were soon on their way to France. Russia's revolution in the same year created a **Bolshevik** regime directed by **Vladimir Lenin (1870-1924)**, who pulled Russia out of the war in March 1918.

A series of desperate German infantry attacks known as "Luddendorff's blows" made considerable headway, but they were stopped by a combination of German exhaustion and the arrival of American troops. By August 1918, the Germans were in retreat, and in October, the Allies penetrated the famous **Hindenburg Line**, on the German border. Kaiser **Wilhelm II** abdicated and the war ended on November 11, 1918 with the signing of the **Versailles Peace Treaty**.

Millions of men had been killed or wounded, vast areas of territory had been wrecked, and four empires had ceased to exist: the Russian empire, dating back to 1618; the German empire founded in 1871; the Austro-Hungarian empire; and the Ottoman empire, which finally lost its hold on the crossroads between Europe and the Middle East.

The creation of the first Communist state in the world created a panic among the western democracies; British statesmen such as **Winston Churchill (1874-1965)** called for the west to strangle Bolshevism in its crib. What the western leaders did not realize was that the average Russian much preferred the dictatorship of the proletariat to the continuation of Czarist rule.

The Czarist regime of **Nicholas II (1868-1918)** entered **World War I** (see no. 81) with an army that had hardly updated its equipment since the **Crimean War** (see no. 66). The first three years of WWI were devastating for Russia, which lost roughly three million men killed, wounded or missing. Spontaneous outbreaks of student and workers' riots occurred in **Petrograd** on March 8, 1917. Czar Nicholas II, who was near the front, ordered soldiers to put down the revolt, but the men refused to fire on their countrymen. Soldiers in **Moscow** mutinied on March 10, and the police who were sent to quell the mutiny were slain. Seeing the hopelessness of the situation, Nicholas abdicated, and a provisional government was set up under **Prince Georgi Lvov**.

Well informed as to the state of affairs in Russia, high ranking German officials decided to allow a dissident author, **Vladimir I. Lenin (1870-1924)** to leave Switzerland and arrive in Petrograd, where he began to motivate the people to revolt. Inciting crowds in chants of "all power to the Soviets" (worker's councils), Lenin found himself at odds with **Alexander F. Kerensky (1881-1970)**, new leader of the provisional government. Ironically, the two men had grown up in the same city, of Simbirsk. Lenin tried to spark a coup, but his premature effort failed and he went into exile again, in Finland. Kerensky made the mistake of trying to continue the Russian involvement in World War I. When the news of further Russian casualties arrived in Petrograd, his government began to lose momentum.

Lenin's closest colleague, **Leon Trotsky (1879-1940)**, organized the November 1917 Revolution that ousted Kerensky from power. On November 6, Kerensky sent troops to shut down the Bolshevik press in Petrograd, but the **Red Guards** struck back and took possession of the state buildings and public utilities. Kerensky fled abroad, and Lenin became president of a **Council of People's Commissioners**. Bolshevik troops took Moscow after bloody street fighting, and within a month, they controlled most of the country. In January 1918, Lenin dissolved the freely elected national assembly, the last open legislature Russia would have until the 1990s.

Lenin addressing a Moscow crowd

Mao Tse-Tung

The long civil war that divided China into the **Nationalist** and **Communist** camps began in 1930, when the Nationalist (Kuomintang) government under Generalissimo **Chiang Kai-shek (1887-1975)** initiated a campaign to eradicate the Communist influence in China. Chiang Kai-shek led five campaigns from 1930 to 1934, trying to encircle Communist strongholds centered in the **Jing Gang** mountain range in the south of China. Following a furious battle at **Goaxing** (in which the Nationalists claimed victory), the Red Army moved its bases farther south. Using tactics gleaned from German advisers, Chiang Kai-shek carried out a scorched earth campaign in 1933, which finally dislodged the Communists from their bases.

In October 1934, 200,000 Communist troops, led by **Mao Tse-Tung (1893-1976)** and **Chou-en-Lai (1898-1976)**, began what would be called the "Long March," a 6,000-mile trek to the north. During the next year, the retreating Communists crossed 18 mountain ranges and 24 major rivers in their movement to safety in the north. After traveling through **Hunan, Kweichow**, and **Szechwan**, the 50,000 survivors of the march arrived in **Shensi** in northern China, where they were soon joined by another 50,000 volunteers.

During the years of the **Sino-Japanese War** (see no. 87), the Communists held control in the north, and Chiang Kai-Shek's Nationalists maintained their position in central and southern China. When **World War II** (see no. 88) ended in 1945, both Nationalists and Communists tried to occupy the areas that were vacated by the Japanese. United States planes assisted the Nationalists by conducting airlifts that allowed them to gain hold of many of the major cities in 1945.

United States General **George Marshall (1880-1959)** sought to mediate between the Nationalists and Communists in 1946; Mao Tse-Tung seemed willing to bargain, but Chiang Kai-shek was not; when Marshall and the last American troops went home in 1947, the **Chinese Civil War** resumed in earnest.

The Communists captured 300,000 Nationalist troops in Manchuria on October 1948 and 66 Nationalist divisions surrendered in northern China in December 1948. The Communists moved south of the Yangtze River for the first time in April 1949, and by December of that year, Chiang Kai-shek and many of his Nationalist followers had fled to the island of **Formosa** (present-day Taiiwan). Mao Tse-Tung set up the **People's Republic of China** in 1949 and Chiang Kai-shek proclaimed the **Republic of China** on Formosa in 1950. One of the longest and most bitter wars of the twentieth century ended with the creation of two Chinas, one mainland and Communist, the other island-based and capitalist.

84. ITALIAN-ETHIOPIAN WAR
1935-1936

What seemed like a sideshow war actually initiated a period of **Fascist** aggression in Europe that led to the outbreak of **World War II** only four years later. **Benito Mussolini (1883-1945)**, the Fascist leader of Italy, had long vowed to take revenge for what had been one of the great defeats of Italian history: loss of

Commission which framed The League of Nations

the **Battle of Adowa** to the Ethiopians in 1896. What should have stopped Mussolini, or any other would-be aggressor during the 1930s, was the presence of the **League of Nations**, created by the **Versailles Treaty** in the aftermath of **World War I**. The brainchild of American President **Woodrow Wilson (1856-1924)**, the League was intended to solve international disputes and prevent acts of aggression by stronger nations against weaker ones.

Mussolini managed to persuade the League that Italy had a right to Ethiopia. Altering treaty documents that had been signed in 1887, 1896 and 1900, he demonstrated that Italy had legitimate interests in the African country that lay next to Italian Somaliland. The League devised the **Hoare-Laval Plan** which called for a partitioning of Ethiopia. This was summarily rejected by Emperor **Haile Selassie I**, and Mussolini pushed forward with the aggressive move he had been planning all along.

In 1934, a bloody clash between Italian and Ethiopian troops at **Ualual**, on the Ethiopian-Somaliland border ensued. Selassie pulled his men back twenty miles from the

border to demonstrate his desire to keep the peace. Confident by this time that the League of Nations would not intervene, Mussolini ordered an Italian invasion that began on October 3, 1935. Using aircraft and modern weaponry, the Italians fought against Ethiopians whose only weapons were horses and spears. The resistance was fierce and it was not until May 5, 1936, that the Italians entered **Addis Ababa**, capital of Ethiopia.

Selassie fled the country and went before the League of Nations in person to plead his nation's cause. The League had already cut off supplies to Italy that would assist the war effort, but it was powerless to take further action, and Selassie went into exile. Italy annexed Ethiopia and joined it with Eritrea and Italian Somaliland to create a new province called **Italian East Africa**.

Mussolini had cleverly combined a show of faith to the letter of international law with a bold defiance of the spirit of that law. Mussolini is thought of as a military and political failure, yet he stood tall in the Fascist world in the 1930s. His actions in Ethiopia served to encourage similar forms of aggression by Nazi Germany.

SPANISH CIVIL WAR
1936-1939

Francisco Franco

The Bourbon monarchy of Spain ended with the reign of King **Alfonso XIII**; Spain became a republic in 1931. Political power was at first held by a centrist coalition, but traditional enmity between the Spanish right and left, combined with economic misery created by the Great Depression of the 1930s, polarized Spanish society. In 1936, the country plunged into a civil war.

General **Francisco Franco (1892-1975)**, leader of the rightist **Falange** group, flew to Spanish **Morocco** and started a revolt in the army barracks there on July 17, 1936. That spark traveled to mainland Spain, where army units revolted at Cadiz, Seville, Bourgos, Saragossa and Huesca. Calling themselves the Spanish **Nationalists**, Franco's followers soon won control of southern and southwestern Spain.

Those who supported the republic labeled themselves the **Loyalists**. Holding northern and central Spain, they nonetheless found themselves fighting on the defensive against the Nationalists, who unified their gains by seizing Badajoz on August 15. **Madrid** itself held out only through a combination of Loyalists and an **International Brigade** of volunteers who had come from Britain, France and the U.S.

On October 1, 1936, Franco was named "Chief of the Spanish State," an ambiguous title that hinted at the type of authoritarian, even Fascist rule, to which he aspired. Franco was soon assisted by German equipment and Italian troops (as many as 70,000 Italians fought in the war), while the Soviet Union sent assistance to the Loyalists. Some 27 other nations agreed to observe neutrality.

The Nationalists moved relentlessly, capturing Bilbao on June 18, 1937 after an eighty-day siege, and Barcelona on January 26, 1939. Madrid surrendered unconditionally on March 28, 1939 after a siege of 28 months, and soon the Nationalist forces had triumphed throughout all of Spain. Britain, France and the United States were forced to recognize Franco's regime.

Despite international pleas for moderation, the Nationalists set up special Fascist tribunals that tried, convicted and executed many Loyalists. The atrocities that had been committed by both sides during the war created a lasting bitterness among the Spanish people, one that held Spain back from fully participating in European affairs until the death of Franco in 1975 and the ascension to the throne of King **Juan Carlos**.

In January 1933, when **Adolf Hitler (1889-1945)** became the chancellor of Germany, the nation was in profound crisis. Nine million Germans were unemployed; the country had been devastated by **World War I** (see no. 81) and the terms of the **Versailles Treaty**; and the runaway inflation of 1923 had reduced the German mark to a small fraction of its earlier value. Hitler promised the German people he would put them back to work and right the wrongs visited upon them by the Versailles Treaty.

Hitler reemployed many Germans by stepping up the armaments industries, and broke the terms of the Versailles Treaty by expanding the size of the army to well over 100,000 men. He then turned an aggressive eye on the territories that had been stripped from Germany by the treaty, knowing that any move he made would likely be countered by the British and French.

In 1936, German troops entered the **Rhineland** area, which had been demilitarized since 1918. Britain and France both protested the action, but neither country took any action. It seemed Hitler really was the Fuhrer, the great leader who could return them to their former status in the European world.

Hitler then sought to reclaim his own true homeland: **Austria**. The Versailles Treaty had specifically forbade any future union between Germany and Austria, but Hitler counted on the sentiments of the Austrian people. In 1937, German tanks and troops entered Austria, where they were greeted with flowers and parades.

In 1938, Hitler began to demand that the eastern sec-

tion of **Czechoslovakia** be given to Germany. The **Sudetenland** contained many German-speaking people, and it also was the strongest and most well-fortified section of Czechoslovakia. By the fall of 1938, the situation had reached a crisis point, and British Prime Minister **Neville Chamberlain (1869-1940)** flew twice to Munich, Germany, to confer in person with Hitler. Declaring that this was his "last territorial demand" in Europe, Hitler alternately intimidated and charmed Chamberlain. The Prime Minister returned to England with an agreement that guaranteed "peace for our time." Many British people, including **Winston Churchill (1874-1965)**, were skeptical, but very few were ready to risk plunging the country and Europe into another world war.

In March 1938, German troops entered and took the rest of Czechoslovakia. By mid-1939, the leaders of Britain and France had changed their minds about Hitler and the potential menace of Nazi Germany. Both Britain and France issued guarantees to Poland that they would ensure its safety from Nazi aggression, but those promises meant little since all of Europe had witnessed Hitler's success at intimidating the European powers into the policy of "appeasement."

Entry of German police into Imst, Austria

A long and deadly war between the two strongest powers in Eastern Asia began in 1937, and depleted the energy each would bring to **World War II** (see no. 88). By 1937, Japan had gained an upper hand in its relationship to Nationalist China, dominated by the government of **Chiang Kai-shek**. Japan had installed **Henry Pu'yi (1906-1967)** (the last Manchu emperor of China, who had been forced to abdicate his throne in 1912) as a puppet emperor in **Manchukuo**, Japanese-dominated Manchuria. Seeking to extend its influence even further, Japan made cautious probes of the northernmost Chinese provinces.

In July 1937, an incident between Japanese and Chinese troops at the **Marco Polo Bridge**, north of Peking, provided the fuel for Japan to invade China. Shots were exchanged at the bridge, and an undeclared war began between **Imperial Japan** and **Nationalist China**.

From the beginning, Japan enjoyed great material superiority. Bombers from Manchukuo attacked the northern Chinese cities, and the Japanese fleet bombed the harbor and city of **Shanghai**. In December 1937, the capital city of **Nanking** fell to the Japanese who proceeded to carry out the infamous "rape of Nanking"; for weeks, the Japanese looted, burned, tortured and raped. The Chinese nationalist government fled to **Hankow**, which was declared the new capital, but when that too fell, the center of government was moved to **Chunking**, in western China. By the end of 1938, the Japanese had occupied all the major coastal cities, and controlled the railroads of eastern China. Considering the population disparity between the two nations, it was a significant military accomplishment.

A stalemate followed during the years 1939 to 1941, and then in December 1941, the Japanese bombed **Pearl Harbor**, bringing the United States into World War II. From that time on, things began to sour for the Japanese. American planes flew **over the hump** of the Himalayas from India to Chunking, delivering supplies and war material to the Nationalists, and the newly trained Chinese air force began to bomb Japanese strongholds in eastern China. Japan could neither occupy the whole of the country, nor induce any Chinese to serve in a puppet government. The end of World War II spelled the doom of the Japanese war effort in China, and the Russian entry into the war brought an invasion that conquered Manchuria for Soviet Russia. By the time the Japanese officially surrendered to the United States on September 2, 1945, many of the coastal areas of China had already been retaken by the Chinese nationalists.

Supplies being transported over the Hump

On September 1, 1939, German soldiers and tanks entered **Poland** using the **Blitzkreig** (lightning warfare) tactics that would make them famous. The soldiers of the German Wehrmacht overran Poland and added that territory to the new **Third Reich** that **Adolf Hitler (1889-1945)** envisioned. France and Britain soon declared war on Germany, and **World War II** began.

In the spring of 1940, German tanks, planes, jeeps and troops overran the Netherlands, Belgium and France. The German **Luftwaffe** (air force) prepared the way by heavy bombing; German tanks and jeeps then broke through the enemy lines, and the mass of German soldiers came last. By July 1940, Hitler stood at the apex of his career; he had come much farther than German Kaiser **Wilhelm II** had ever managed to achieve in all the years of **World War I** (see no. 81).

Hitler's first setback came in the fall of 1940 when Britain refused to submit to his aerial bombardment. The fighter pilots of the **Royal Air Force** eventually gained the upper hand against the Luftwaffe. Hitler soon turned his attention against Russia, launching the invasion of that country in "Operation Barbarossa", named for Emperor **Frederick Barbarossa** of the former Holy Roman Empire (see no. 25), in June 1941.

The early German attacks yielded tremendous success. Millions of Russians were killed or wounded, as Hitler's armies drove toward Moscow. They were finally halted by Russian troops brought in from Siberia, in company with the bitter cold winter of 1941. At almost the same time, Hitler's Japanese ally chose to launch a surprise attack against the United States Naval base at **Pearl Harbor**, thus bringing America into the war.

From that moment on, the **Axis** powers (Germany, Italy and Japan) were doomed. Although many epic battles remained to be fought, and German resilience on the battlefield caused much anxiety to the **Allied** war commanders, the combined industrial strength and manpower of Britain, the United States and the Soviet Union could not be denied. Hitler did succeed in maintaining the initiative in the war until the twin defeats of **Stalingrad** in February 1943 and **North Africa** in March 1943, combined with the Japanese defeat at **Midway** in June 1942 to hand momentum to the Allied powers.

In 1944, Russian armies threw the Germans out of Russia and advanced as far as Warsaw, Poland, while American, British and Canadian soldiers stormed ashore at **Normandy** and opened the way for the liberation of France. Hitler mustered large forces for a last counterattack in the Ardennes forest area, but the ensuing **Battle of the Bulge** ended his attempt. By late April 1945, Hitler had committed suicide in his bunker, and the European war was at an end. The war went on in the Pacific theater until August 1945, when two atomic bombs, exploded over **Hiroshima** and **Nagasaki**, persuaded the Japanese to surrender.

Little Boy

89. COLD WAR
1945-1990

Hardly had the elation over defeating Hitler ended than the **United States** and **Soviet Union** found themselves moving in opposite directions: one wanted to make the world safe for democracy and capitalism, while the other sought to convert the world to a socialist society based on Marxist-Leninist doctrine.

It was during the governments of **Josef Stalin (1879-1953)** and American President **Harry Truman (1884-1972)** that the **Cold War** began. The Soviet Union quickly gained control of nearly all of central and eastern Europe at the end of **World War II** (see no. 88), and when Russia sent assistance to Communist guerrilla fighters in Greece, Truman responded with the **Truman Doctrine** and policy of containment, which stated the United States would assist any government that sought to defend itself from Communist aggression. In 1946, former British Prime Minister **Winston Churchill (1874-1965)** noted that an "Iron Curtain" had descended upon central and eastern Europe, thus coining a phrase that became emblematic of the Cold War. In 1949, the United States was instrumental in the forming of **NATO** (North Atlantic Treaty Organization) for the defense of western Europe, and Russia responded with the **Warsaw Pact** of 1955.

The Russians blockaded West Berlin (held by the Americans) from 1948 to 1949; only a massive American airlift campaign deterred the Soviets. American President **Dwight Eisenhower (1890-1969)** twice intimated he might use nuclear weapons in **Vietnam**, but it was under his successor **John F. Kennedy (1917-1963)** that the largest crisis came to pass. In 1962, Kennedy demanded the Soviets withdraw their missiles from the island of **Cuba**. Soviet premier **Nikita Khruschev (1894-1971)** demurred at first, and the world came within hours of the American-imposed deadline before the Russians backed away from the crisis. In 1973, the United States and Soviet Union both seemed ready to enter the Middle East to back up their client states during the **Yom Kippur War** (see no. 97).

The American-Russian rivalry eased during the detente era of the 1970s, but returned with a vengeance during the presidency of **Ronald Reagan (b. 1911)**, who initiated a **Strategic Defense Initiative** that he believed would render the United States invulnerable to a nuclear attack. In their efforts to keep up with American technology, the Russians spent what was left of their economic resources, and during the leadership of **Mikhail Gorbachov (b. 1931)**, the Kremlin turned away from confrontation. Declaring a policy of "glasnost" (openness), Gorbachov met with Reagan and his successor **George Bush (b. 1924)** and greatly reduced the number of Soviet missiles pointed toward the United States.

It was the revolutions of 1989 in eastern and central Europe that provided the death blow to the Cold War. Russia did not intervene when East Germany, Hungary, Romania and other countries ousted their Communist governments, and the Iron Curtain fell in late 1989. Russia itself soon entered the throes of change and by 1991, both Gorbachov and Bush spoke of the end of the Cold War and the start of cooperation between east and west.

Nikita Khruschev and John F. Kennedy

The war between France and part of its former colony that began in 1946 turned into a war with international repercussions; one that convinced many French of the futility of trying to maintain an overseas empire. In 1946, France, elated over having been freed from Nazi occupation, sought to reestablish itself as one of the significant colonial powers of the world.

Japan withdrew its forces from **Indochina** in 1945, and two Indochinas soon emerged. **The Democratic Republic of Vietnam** was proclaimed on September 2, 1946, with the city of **Hanoi** as the capital and **Ho Chi Minh (1890-1969)** as the first president. Wary of the upstart state, the French organized a provisional government in the southern part of the country, under the nominal rule of Emperor **Bao Dai**, but it was in reality a French puppet state.

On December 19, 1946, Vietminh forces (North Vietnam) launched a surprise attack on French installations near Hanoi, inaugurating a struggle that would last for the next seven years. The French resisted any compromise with North Vietnam, and gained reluctant United States recognition of their **Associated State of Vietnam**, with its capital located at **Saigon**, in the southern part of what had formerly been Indochina.

Under the leadership of Ho Chi Minh and General **Vo Nguyen Giap**, the North Vietnamese launched an offensive in the Red River Delta in 1950 that failed to dislodge the French. Between 1951 and 1953, the Vietminh harassed the French with guerrilla warfare to such an extent that popular support for the struggle began to diminish in France itself. The key to undermining the last French resistance came when the Vietnamese besieged French-held **Dien Bien Phu** in the northwest part of French Vietnam. The siege occurred from March 13 to May 7, 1954,

French Foreign Legionnaire

directed by General Giap, who astounded his enemies by bringing artillery through what many believed was impassable terrain, and disguising his approach until he was ready to launch a series of all-out attacks.

Even though the French inflicted heavy casualties, the relentless human wave assaults and artillery bombardments wore the defenders down. The French surrendered on May 7, marking the end of an era in European colonialism: not even the airpower and firepower of the French had been able to save the fortress from capture by a relentless enemy that was determined to gain and hold its own country. An armistice was signed in July 1954, temporarily dividing Vietnam between northern and southern parts at the **17th parallel**. The French soon left Vietnam, leaving the path open for another Western power to test its will and strength against that of Communist North Vietnam.

Mohandas Gandhi

The sudden independence of India, gained in 1947, led to rejoicing on the part of Indians who had worked with **Mohandas Karamchand Gandhi (1869-1948)** to gain the country's freedom. Yet India's internal and external problems remained in force. These problems were especially difficult since they involved both religious and territorial issues.

Given the division on the subcontinent between **Hindus** and **Muslims**, Britain and the United Nations decided to partition India into two states: predominantly **Hindu India**, and **East** and **West Pakistan**. East and West Pakistan lay hundreds of miles apart, separated by the bulk of northern India. The partition went into effect August 14, 1947, and Britain officially withdrew its presence from the subcontinent.

Almost at once, on August 16, a civil war between Hindus and Muslims broke out in the **Punjab** of India. The fighting soon spread, and both Hindus and Muslims in the northern area panicked. Five and a half million refugees switched places between West Pakistan and western India, some 1.25 mil-

lion fled from East Pakistan to West Benghal, and 400,000 Hindus left West Pakistan for India. Rioting was constant in all the northern areas, and perhaps one million people died between 1947 and 1948 during the period of dislocation. The first prime minister of India, **Jawaharal Nehru (1889-1964)**, did not allow the British troops still in India to intervene, making the riots more difficult to subdue.

The former British Indian state of **Jammu-Kashmir** had elected to maintain independence from both India and Pakistan. The predominantly Muslim population was ruled by a class of Hindu landlords, and in October 1947, Pathan Muslims in Poonch revolted against the landowners. Since Jammu-Kashmir bordered on both Pakistan and India, Pakistan sent troops in to defend the rights of the Muslim population. The Pakistani forces seized **Muzaffarabad** and **Uri**, burned a number of villages, and advanced to within sight of the capital of **Srinigar**. The ruler of Jammu-Kashmir appealed for Indian assistance, and Indian troops were airlifted from Delhi to Kashmir. The Indian troops (Sikhs for the most part) pushed the Pakistanis back to their own border with Kashmir.

On January 30, 1948, Gandhi was assassinated by a Hindu extremist. Gandhi had worked, fasted and prayed for peace between Hindus and Muslims, and in the aftermath of his death, the Hindus and Muslims within India came to better terms with each other. Three more weeks of fighting between India and Pakistan in Kashmir led to a United Nations ceasefire in April 1948. Most of Kashmir became a state of India, while the part that was still held by Pakistan became a province of that country known as Azad (free) Kashmir. Disputes over water rights between Pakistan and India continued until 1960.

92. ISRAELI WAR OF INDEPENDENCE
1948-1949

The Jewish state of **Israel** was proclaimed on May 14, 1948. On that same day, the armies and air forces of five different Arab states (**Egypt, Syria, Transjordan, Lebanon,** and **Iraq**) declared war on the new nation. The Israelis quickly adopted the motto of "Ein B'reira" (No other solution), and their fight for survival created a military ethic that has seldom been equaled in the history of warfare.

Israel was created through the work of the **United Nations**; they were trying to give recompense to the Jews for the profound losses they had endured during **World War II** (see no. 88). The United Nations partition of **Palestine** left half the land in the hands of the Palestinians and half in the hands of the Israelis, who by 1948 numbered around 600,000.

The war began with Arab planes bombing Jewish towns, and the armies of all five Arab nations attacking Israel at once. The situation looked absolutely hopeless, since the Arabs had both an overwhelming superiority in numbers and better military equipment. The Israelis fought back; their mission was to preserve their new homeland, the first they had had since the taking of Jerusalem and Judea by the Romans (see no. 14). The Transjordanian troops captured the **Old City of Jerusalem**, and the Arab forces were halted everywhere else by the time a U.N. truce took effect on June 11.

When the fighting resumed on July 8, it was the Israelis who took the offensive, capturing **Nazareth** (but not the Old City of Jerusalem). A second truce, begun on July 18, allowed the Arabs to regroup. Fighting broke out again on October 14, with yet another truce instituted on October 22. The last campaign of the war was fought between December 22 and January 8, 1949. By this time the overall strength of the Israeli army

had reached 100,000 men and women, and the Jews pushed the Arabs back on all fronts.

The ceasefire of January 7, 1949 led to negotiations that finally ended in July 1949, with Israel signing armistices with all the Arab nations except Iraq, which did, however, withdraw its forces from the field. By the late summer of 1949, there was no doubt that the new Israeli nation had survived its first major test; through tremendous resourcefulness and determination.

Jewish children on their way to Israel

On June 25, 1950, **North Korean** troops crossed the **38th parallel** of north latitude and attacked the **Republic of South Korea**. Two days later, the **United Nations** called on its members to assist the beleaguered South Koreans; 15 countries responded immediately. The United States was foremost among the United Nations members, and when the U.N. asked President **Harry Truman (1884-1972)** to designate the commander-in-chief for the operation, he quickly named General **Douglas MacArthur (1880-1964)** to the post.

The North Koreans captured ground with a terrifying rapidity, and by August 5, they had nearly reached the southern tip of the peninsula. There they were held by a combination of South Korean and U.N. forces, on the line of the **Pusan Perimeter**. General MacArthur designed a risky amphibious movement that would allow him to outflank the enemy who had over-extended their supply lines.

On September 15, 1950, U.N. troops landed hundreds of miles behind the North Korean lines at **Inchon**, on the shore of the Yellow Sea. The U.N. units went ashore and liberated the capital city of **Seoul**. The North Koreans panicked at the move, particularly when the U.N. troops in the Pusan Perimeter broke out. The southern forces were able to push the entire North Korean army back to the 38th parallel of north latitude within a

matter of days. MacArthur made an important decision to carry the war into North Korea, and by November 25, 1950, some U.N. troops had actually reached the Yalu River, the border between North Korea and Manchurian China.

On the evening of November 25, thousands of **Chinese** troops crossed the Yalu, and attacked the U.N. troops, pushing them southwards. MacArthur urged his superiors in Washington D.C. to bomb the Chinese airfields and supply depots, but President Truman and his closest advisors wanted to confine the war to Korean soil. The U.N. troops were pushed back to a line about fifty miles south of Seoul, where they managed to hold the Chinese-Korean offensive.

On March 24, 1951, MacArthur issued a statement threatening the Chinese with devastation if they did not withdraw from Korea. Other intemperate statements followed, and on April 11, 1951, President Truman relieved MacArthur of his command, replacing him with General **Matthew Ridgway**.

In June 1951, the "talking war" began. U.N. and Korean diplomats discussed issues of withdrawal and prisoner exchanges. It was not until the start of 1953 that much progress was made in the talks--**Dwight Eisenhower (1890-1969)** became U.S. President in January, and he hinted that he might use nuclear weapons to end the war. In March 1953, Soviet leader **Josef Stalin (1897-1953)** died, and the Communist leadership decided to consolidate its position rather than risk new ventures. The **Armistice of Panmunjom** was signed on July 27, 1953, leaving the two countries where they had started the war, at the 38th parallel. No peace treaty was ever signed to formally conclude the war that cost 520,000 North Korean, 900,000 Chinese, 1,300,000 South Korean, 54,246 American, and 3,360 United Nations casualties.

Crossing the 38th Parallel

Between 1956 and 1959, a tiny handful of guerrilla fighters led by **Fidel Castro (b. 1926)**, ousted the military regime of General **Fulgencio Batista y Zaldivar (1901-1973)**. Carried out by the most slender of means, the **Cuban Revolution** created the first Communist state in the Western hemisphere, provoking anger from its neighbor to the north.

Fidel Castro was both an excellent athlete and student as a young man; he earned a law degree in 1950. On July 26, 1953, he led 160 revolutionaries in a suicidal attack on the Moncada army post in Santiago de Cuba. Captured and sentenced to fifteen years in prison, he actually served only two years before he was released in a general amnesty. With a handful of followers, he went to Mexico to plan his next attempt at unseating Batista, who himself had taken power in a coup in 1952.

Castro and 81 followers landed on the coast of the province of Oriente on December 2, 1956, following a harrowing seven-day voyage from Mexico aboard the yacht Granma. Units of Batista's Rural Guard struck Castro's men on December 5, killing or capturing all but **Che Guevara**, 14 men, and Castro himself. Seeing how desperate his position was, Castro led his tiny band into the **Sierra Maestra** mountain range.

At the start of his fight against Batista, Castro had 16 men to combat 40,000 troops and police. On January 17, 1957, Castro won his first victory at the tiny **Battle of La Plata**; small though it was, the battle inaugurated the fame of Castro's guerrilla force. After barely surviving an aerial attack against his position two weeks later, Castro issued his "Appeal to the People of Cuba," which outlined proposals for the improvement of Cuban society.

Batista sent thousands of men against Castro's mountain position in a 76-day offensive starting on May 20, 1957. Batista lost a thousand men killed and 400 taken prisoner, while Castro became a hero to the Cuban population. Making endless broadcasts on **Radio Rebelde**, Castro condemned Batista and his regime as corrupt and spineless. In 1957, Castro's brother, **Raul Castro**, seized 49 United States citizens; the older brother quickly released the hostages and actually gained ground in Cuba as a result.

Castro achieved his breakthrough success at the end of 1958. Che Guevara captured the key city of **Santa Clara** on December 30, and just after midnight on December 31, Batista and his family boarded planes to flee to the Dominican Republic. Castro entered Santiago on January 2, and **Havana** itself on January 3, 1959. His remarkable revolution had taken 25 months; in the following eighteen months he would lead Cuba toward its present-day status as a Marxist-Leninist state. Though many observers criticize Castro's methods and economic failures, he remains a world leader with one of the longest tenures on record in the twentieth century.

Fidel Castro

101

VIETNAM WAR
1956-1975

In 1956 a civil war began between the Communist government of **North Vietnam** (established in 1946), and the government of **South Vietnam**, which was increasingly backed by the United States. Originally, it was a guerrilla war fought by **Viet Cong** soldiers, men who returned to their homes in South Vietnam to fight against the nominally democratic government.

From the start, the United States provided military advisers to South Vietnam, and in 1961, President **John F. Kennedy (1917-1963)** authorized those advisers to fight alongside the South Vietnamese troops. By the time of his assassination in November 1963, Kennedy had increased the U.S. presence in Vietnam to a sizeable 16,000 men.

It was left to his successor, President **Lyndon B. Johnson (1908-1972)**, to expand the American commitment. On August 2, 1964, North Vietnamese patrol boats allegedly attacked American destroyers in the **Gulf of Tonkin**. Johnson increased the size of American forces in Vietnam, without an official declaration of war. American planes conducted bombing raids of North Vietnam, and American troops were sent as official allies, no longer as advisers. By 1968, there were over half a million American troops in Vietnam, conducting search and destroy missions against the Viet Cong.

In January 1968, North Vietnam launched its **Tet Offensive**, striking 36 cities in South Vietnam. Though the North Vietnamese were driven off with heavy losses, their determination and courage astounded observers, and antiwar sentiment began to grow in the United States.

President Johnson did not run for reelection in 1968 and his successor, **Richard M. Nixon (1913-1994)**, began to withdraw troops from South Vietnam in May 1969. By December 1971, the number of Americans in Vietnam was down to 184,000.

North Vietnam launched an invasion across the **17th parallel** in 1972, and seized a northern province. In retaliation, the United States mined the major harbors of North Vietnam. Peace talks, which had begun in 1968, dragged on without progress, and in December 1972, President Nixon ordered eleven days of bombing against the cities of North Vietnam. A ceasefire in January 1973 led to accusations of bad faith on both sides. In 1974, North Vietnam captured several provincial capitals of South Vietnam, and in January 1975, North Vietnam launched the long-dreaded full-scale invasion of the south, through the central highlands. On April 30, 1975, South Vietnam surrendered unconditionally to Communist North Vietnam, and **Saigon** was renamed **Ho Chi Minh City**.

United as the **Socialist Republic of Vietnam** on July 2, 1976, the new country basked in its defeat of French and American imperialists over a thirty-year period. Since 1956, South Vietnam had 220,357 killed and 499,000 wounded, North Vietnam lost 444,000, and the United States reported 57,605 killed and 303,700 wounded.

U.S. troops crossing a jungle river

In June 1967, the relatively small army and air force of **Israel** conducted one of the most lopsided campaigns in the history of warfare. Starting from the premise that they had to win completely or face destruction, the Israelis planned and executed a military masterpiece between June 5 and June 10.

Egyptian President **Gamel Abdel Nasser (1918-1970)**, generally recognized as the most prominent leader in the Arab world, called for United Nations (U.N.) forces to leave Egypt in May 1967. The U.N. complied, and Nasser soon instituted a shipping blockade of the **Strait of Tiran**, cutting off Israel's port in the **Gulf of Aquaba**. As other Arab countries began to mass their armies, the world looked on in a state of suspended animation. The Jewish victories in 1948 to 1949 and 1956 seemed to fade in comparison with the combined forces set against them in the spring of 1967.

Surprisingly, Israel struck first. At 7:10 a.m. on the morning of June 5, 1967, Israeli warplanes took off, and by 7:45 a.m. were flying over the airfields of the Egyptian air force. Two other waves followed the first, and in three hours the Israelis had destroyed 300 of the 340 planes of the Egyptian air force. Similar attacks were launched against **Jordan** and **Syria**; by the end of the day, Israel had eliminated 416 enemy planes, 393 of them on the ground. The Israelis themselves had lost 26 planes, all to antiaircraft fire.

That same morning, Israeli forces attacked on the ground, starting at 8:15 a.m., and met with success in almost every quarter. They routed an Egyptian army of 200,000 men in the **Sinai Desert** and pushed all the way to the eastern bank of the **Suez Canal**. On the eastern front, the Israelis fought hand-to-hand against the Jordanians, and captured both the **Old City of Jerusalem** and the entire **West Bank** of the Jordan River by June 7, depriv-

Gamel Abdel Nasser

ing Jordan of its most fertile land. To the north, the Israelis struck hard against the Syrians, who fought back with desperation, but by June 10, the entire **Golan Heights** (a series of mountains overlooking northern Israel) were in Israeli hands. The war ended with a ceasefire on June 10, 1967.

Israel had greatly expanded its territory and completely reversed the military situation in the Middle East. Prior to 1967, Arab bombers and planes were always close to the Israeli border. After the war, it was Israeli planes, based in the Sinai, on the West Bank, or northern Israel, that could strike almost at will against the Arab capitals of Cairo, Amman, and Damascus. The Israelis lost 759 men and women killed and three times as many wounded, while the Arabs suffered a total of roughly 30,000 men killed, wounded or missing in the war. The remarkable victory was a testament to the meticulous planning of the **Israeli Defense Forces** prior to the war.

Anwar Sadat

When Egyptian and Syrian forces attacked Israel on **Yom Kippur** in 1973, they caught the Israelis off-guard. What followed was another desperate struggle between Arabs and Jews in the Middle East.

President **Anwar Sadat (1918-1981)** of Egypt wanted to avenge the Arab defeats in the **Six Day War** (see no. 96) of 1967. Working in close cooperation with Syrian President **Hafez el-Assad**, Sadat worked out a timetable under which both Egypt and Syria would attack Israel on the holy day of Yom Kippur on October 6, 1973. The Arab states received a great deal of arms and equipment from the Soviet Union, and were ready to carry out an offensive against the Israelis.

The war began with simultaneous attacks on the **Suez Canal** and **Golan Heights**. The Egyptians launched skillful amphibious assaults that took them across the canal in a matter of hours. The Egyptians brought 200,000 men to the **Sinai Desert**, linking up their bridgeheads by October 10. There they paused, jubilant over their success, but not yet daring to test it by forcing the Milta and Giddi passes through the desert.

Meanwhile, the Syrians struck with a vengeance on the Golan Heights. Heedless of the number of tanks and men lost, the Syrians pushed forward, and by October 8 had reclaimed most of the territory. Only Israel's remarkable capacity to mobilize its armed forces rapidly saved the entire heights from being overrun.

The Israelis decided upon a "Sinai first" strategy. On October 12 to 14, Egyptian and Israeli armor met in an enormous tank battle in the Sinai, second in size only to the Russian-German tank battle at **Kursk** in 1943. Although neither side won outright, the standoff ensured that the Egyptians would not press forward. On October 15, 1967, Israeli General **Arik Sharon** led a daring counterattack that took a small Israeli tank force across the canal, behind the Egyptian lines. Had the Egyptians seen the maneuver in time, they could have crushed it, but lacking an early warning, they soon found themselves isolated on the eastern side of the canal, with the entire Egyptian Third Army cut off from supplies. Confident that the war was now in hand, the Israelis struck back against Syria, regaining all the ground the Syrians had taken and more; the Israelis came to within 24 miles of **Damascus**.

The war ended with a ceasefire on October 24. On that same day, United States President **Richard Nixon (1913-1994)** put all American military units on a Defcom B alert (one level below acute alert) in response to reports that the Soviet Union would airlift troops to help the Syrians. The war left 2,552 Israelis dead and 3,000 wounded; the Egyptians suffered 7,700 casualties and the Syrians lost 3,500 men. Both sides could legitimately claim to have gained something; the Arabs reclaimed their pride, while the Israelis could point to their remarkable comeback.

98. AFGHAN CIVIL WAR
1979-1989

In December 1979, Soviet troops and tanks entered **Afghanistan**, starting what the Kremlin believed would be the equivalent of a police action. Instead, the **Soviet Union** entered into what many historians call **Russia's Vietnam**.

The Afghan monarchy was overthrown in 1973, and the **People's Democratic Party** (friendly to the Soviet Union) was soon the only political party allowed expression in Afghanistan. The new government concluded a treaty of friendship with the Soviet Union in December 1978, and Afghanistan was soon flooded with Soviet Communist literature and propaganda. What both the Soviets and the People's Democratic Party had overlooked was the long history of the Afghan tribes resenting and resisting outside influence (see no. 62 and no. 75). The tribal communities revolted against the government in 1979, and the People's Democratic Party showed internal weakness as well; the president was ousted by his prime minister in September 1979, who was himself soon overthrown by the leftist leader **Babrak Karmal**.

Soviet leaders sent 30,000 troops into Afghanistan in the last week of December 1979. Tanks and support units soon followed, and the Soviets soon turned Karmal's cabinet into a puppet government. The initial Soviet success in taking Kabul and other major cities was denounced by many world leaders (U.S. President **Jimmy Carter** among them), but the world's reaction began to shift when it was observed how embarrassing the Afghanistan experience was becoming for the Soviet army.

Known as the **mujahedin** (holy warriors), the Afghan tribesmen fought the Soviets from positions in the countryside. The Soviet tanks could not penetrate the mountain areas, and the guerrilla fighters picked off Soviet troops and soldiers of Karmal's government in large numbers. The Afhgan rebels were soon assisted by arms shipments from both the United States and Communist China; the weapons were funneled to Afghanistan through Pakistan.

Surprised by the strength of the rebel resistance, the Soviet Union sent large numbers of reinforcements, until the total number of Russian troops reached 115,000 men. As the decade of the 1980s advanced, the Soviet leaders found it humiliating to send so many troops and commit so much money to a campaign that wasn't going anywhere. In April 1988, the Soviets accepted a United Nations-brokered agreement for withdrawal, and by February 1989, nearly 10 years after the invasion, the last Russian troops departed from Afghanistan.

The Afghanistan experience contributed to a lowering of Russian prestige in the world, and it was the last military adventure of the Kremlin during the Soviet era. **Mikhail Gorbachov (b. 1931)**, the Soviet leader who carried out the withdrawal, would be the last Soviet leader of the **Cold War**.

Afghan soldier holding captured AK-47 assault rifle

IRAN-IRAQ WAR
1980-1988

The war that began between Iran and Iraq in 1980 had economic, political and religious causes, but it soon proved one of the most fruitless struggles waged in the second half of the twentieth century. Iran, a nation with a majority of **Sh'ite Muslims**, was led by the **Ayatollah Ruhollah Khomeini (1900-1989)**, who had seized power from the secular government of the **Shah** in 1979. Predominantly **Sunni Muslim**, Iraq was led by the dictator **Saddham Hussein (b. 1937)**, leader of the Ba'ath Party. The two leaders detested each other.

Iran and Iraq had long feuded over control of the **Shatt al-Arab River**, which flowed

Ayatollah Ruhollah Khomeini

between the two nations on its way to the Persian Gulf. Iran made the first move in the conflict, targeting both Hussein and his deputy premier for assassination, and attacking the Iraqi embassy in Rome. In response, Iraqi troops and tanks invaded southeastern Iran on September 21 to 22, 1980. Hussein's troops met with initial success; they sank Iranian gunboats in the Shatt al-Arab and caused considerable damage to Iranian airfield and oil refineries.

Khomeini, however, rallied the Iranian people, inspiring them to fight with a reckless abandon almost unknown in the century that had invented tanks, planes, bombs and missiles. Human "waves" of young Iranians attacked Iraqi troops in trenches, armed with machine guns. Despite the enormous casualties the Iranians suffered, their all-out tactics eventually took both a human and psychological toll on their opponents, and by early 1982, Iran had retaken all the ground it had lost earlier to Iraq (the fighting took place in the Iranian provinces of **Khuzestan** and **Kermanshah**).

Making matters worse for Hussein, Israeli planes, in an action not connected to the Iran-Iraq war, bombed and destroyed the Osirak nuclear reactor near Baghdad, where scientists were close to creating an atomic bomb. From 1982 on, Hussein sought to make peace, but the Ayatollah was remorseless, wanting only to destroy the Iraqi leader and regime. The war continued, with both countries suffering an enormous human, material, and economic toll from the war effort and the loss of oil revenues. A ceasefire was agreed to in August 1988. Khomeini died in June 1989, and Hussein had some small reason to claim victory in a war that had cost a million lives and poisoned relations between two of the richest and most powerful Arab countries in the world.

100. PERSIAN GULF WAR
1990-1991

Fought during the winter of 1990 to 1991, the **Persian Gulf War** was the most televised conflict of human history. Millions of television viewers witnessed the use of "smart bombs," Tomahawk cruise missiles, and other technological wonders.

On August 2, 1990, **Iraqi** troops and planes invaded the tiny oil-rich state of **Kuwait**, directly to the south of their own country. By August 8, Iraqi leader **Saddham Hussein (b. 1937)** announced the annexation of Kuwait, and his gamble to increase his oil revenues seemed to have succeeded. Thousands of miles away, American President **George Bush (b. 1924)** announced that Hussein's invasion must be repelled. Working through the **United Nations**, Bush assembled a coalition of countries willing to assist the United States in forcing Iraq to yield the fruits of her aggression. Economic sanctions were put in place on August 6, 1990, and on the next day, Bush announced **Operation Desert Shield**, under which thousands of American military personnel were rushed to the Middle East and deployed in the desert kingdom of **Saudi Arabia**.

American General **H. Norman Schwarzkopf** led the Rapid Deployment Force which numbered 100,000 U.S. troops within 30 days, and 230,000 men by November, 1990. American soldiers were met by troops from other countries that had joined the coalition, and soon the United Nations gave a deadline of January 15, 1991 for an Iraqi withdrawal from Kuwait.

Saddham Hussein refused to retreat; he predicted a conflict that would turn into "the mother of battles." Last-minute talks in Geneva, Switzerland failed to change the Iraqi position, and on the night of January 16, 1991, coalition forces began **Operation Desert Storm** with a devastating aerial bombardment of Iraq itself. "Smart bombs" found

General H. Norman Schwarzkopf

military targets as they avoided civilian centers; 112,000 sorties were launched during the war.

The ground war began on the evening of February 24. American, Saudi Arabian, Egyptian, Syrian, British and French troops made a wide sweeping flanking movement through the desert of Iraq against the Iraqi troops in Kuwait. The Iraqi resistance began to crumble, and soon Hussein's army was in full retreat to the north. The forced retreat was plagued by bombing from the air and thousands of Iraqi tanks, jeeps and personnel carriers were destroyed on the single main road running north from Kuwait. The United States called off the ground war on February 28, after 100 hours of fighting in which the Iraqis had been totally ejected from Kuwait.

The coalition forces lost 343 killed (of whom 268 were American) during the war. The enormous Iraqi losses have been estimated at 100,000 killed, 300,000 wounded, and 88,000 taken prisoner.

TRIVIA QUIZ & GAMES

Test your knowledge and challenge your friends with the following questions. The answers are on the pages noted.

1. This leader originally shared the Frankish kingdom with his brother, Caroloman. After Caroloman's death he led successful campaigns against many nations. However, he failed to penetrate the defenses of one nation. On Christmas Day, 800 AD, he was crowned Emperor of the Romans by Pope Leo. Who was this famous leader and what nation was he unsuccessful at defeating? (see page 25)

2. After first winning an unsteady internal independence, they declared a second war on Great Britain on October 11, 1899 along with their ally, the Orange Free State. The Treaty of Vereeniging provided British sovereignty, but led many English people to say that these people had lost the war but won the peace. Who were these people? (see page 85)

3. This European leader's bold aggression against Ethiopia in 1935 defied international law and the spirit of the League of Nations. His bold actions indirectly encouraged similar forms of aggression by Germany. Who was this cunning leader? (see page 91)

4. Initially a religious war between the Protestant Bohemia and the Catholic Czechoslovakia within the Holy Roman Empire, it eventually consumed most all major European countries. Name the war. (see page 48)

5. Angered at the thought of Jerusalem falling into the hands of the Seljuk Turks, he gave a rousing speech to thousands of French nobles at Clermont, urging the French knights to lead a holy war to reconquer the Middle East. Who was this religious leader and what war did he instigate? (see page 30)

6. The Peloponnesian War dragged on until the land-based Spartans finally developed something of their own with some assistance from the Persians. What did they develop? (see page 10)

7. Captured by the Carthaginians in North Africa, this Roman general was told to begin negotiations. Instead he instructed his fellow Romans to fight on. This display of courage and heroic self-sacrifice gave the Romans their greatest resource. Who was this Roman general? (see page 13)

8. When King Charles I fell into serious conflict with Parliament he tried to dissolve it and arrest its leaders. This led to the English Civil War between two groups - those loyal to the King and those who were loyal to Parliament. Name these two groups and name the leader who emerged as the head of the Parliament group. (see page 49)

9. In the American Civil War, Confederate General Robert E. Less led two invasions of the North. Name two major battles that resulted from these invasions. (see page 78)

10. In the 1890s Spain attempted to put down insurrections in two of its colonial possessions. Influential American newspapers called on the United States to put an end to Spanish control in the Western Hemisphere. Name the two colonies of Spain and the American newspaper

108

publisher who called for U.S. military actions against Spain. (see page 84)

11. With the Vikings breathing down the neck of Paris, Charles the Simple, king of France, made an unusual deal with the Viking leader Rollo. If Rollo would become a Christian and marry one of the king's daughters, then he could hold onto the land they presently occupied. Name the territory in France that this area is known as. (see page 26)

12. His crowning glory came at the Battle of Cannae in 216, when he effected a dou ble envelopment maneuver and trapped some 50,000 Roman soldiers. Name this Carthaginian leader and name the war in which the battle was fought. (see page 14)

13. In 1862 this Prussian Chancellor stated, "The great questions of the day will not be settled by means of speeches and majority decisions, but by iron and blood." Who was this Prussian leader and name the war that he provoked in 1866. (see page 80)

14. Concerned by the insatiable appetite of the early English colonists for land he developed an alliance between his tribe and others in the New England area, planning to rid the area of the English. Name this Native American chief and the war he provoked. (see page 50)

15. Name the city that Attila the Hun laid siege against, resulting in an increase in that city's yearly payment of gold to the Huns from 700 pounds to 2,100 pounds. (see page 22)

16. Name the country that was founded as a result of the War of Peruvian Independence and name the Colombian patriot and revolutionary for which it was named. (see page 63)

17. After failing to gain mutual recognition of interests in two countries, Japan abruptly broke off talks with Czarist Russia. Without a formal declaration of war, Japan made surprise attacks against Russian warships gaining superiority at sea. Name the two countries that Japan and Russia fought over and name the treaty negotiated by U.S. President Theodore Roosevelt. (see page 86)

SUGGESTED PROJECTS

1. Many of the wars discussed in this book describe both strategies and tactics used by the opposing forces. Describe the differ- ence between a strategy and a tactic. Find three examples of each in the book.

2. Military leaders often try to find the strengths and weakness of an opponent in order to gain an advanatge. Choose a part- ner. Each partner chooses a different country. Each partner then makes a list of the others strengths and weaknesses and chooses one weakness to attack. Compare lists and discuss the possible outcome.

INDEX